# Psychoanalysis in an Age of Accelerating Cultural Change

## Spiritual Globalization

*Psychoanalysis in an Age of Accelerating Cultural Change: Spiritual Globalization* addresses the current status of mental health work in the public and private sectors. The careful, thorough, approach to the individual person characteristic of psychoanalysis is mostly the province of an affluent few. Meanwhile, community-based mental health treatment, given shrinking budgets, tends to emphasize medication and short-term therapies. In an increasingly diverse society, considerations of culture in mental health treatment are given short shrift, despite obligatory nods to cultural competence.

The field of mental health has suffered from the mutual isolation of psychoanalysis, community-based clinical work, and cultural studies. Here, Neil Altman shows how these areas of study and practice require and enrich each other – the field of psychoanalysis benefits by engaging marginalized communities; community-based clinical work benefits from psychoanalytic concepts, while all forms of clinical work benefit from awareness of culture. Including reports of clinical experiences and programmatic developments from around the world, its international scope explores the operation of culture and cultural differences in conceptions of mental health. In addition the book addresses the origin and treatment of mental illness, from notions of spirit possession treated by shamans, to conceptions of psychic trauma, to biological understandings and pharmacological treatments. In the background of this discussion is globalization, the impact of which is tracked in terms of its psychological effects on people, as well as on the resources and programs available to provide psychological care around the world.

As a unique examination of current mental health work, this book will appeal to psychoanalysts, psychotherapists, community-based mental health workers, and students in Cultural Studies.

**Neil Altman** is a psychoanalytic psychologist, Visiting Professor at Ambedkar University of Delhi, India, and faculty and supervisor at the William Alanson White Institute. He is an Honorary Member of the William Alanson White Society and Editor Emeritus of *Psychoanalytic Dialogues*.

Altman's book opens our minds to the new cultural and social scenario marked by globalization where mental health professionals work and live today. His deep knowledge of cultural differences and their impact on our lives is now contextualized from his experience both in clinical and community settings. Contemporary psychoanalysis is not only a matter of office based practice, but has opened to the community, and as he says, needs to be practiced there if it is to survive with much social relevance, overcomig its roots in elitism and isolation. Facing a present focus on 'evidence based treatments', Altman gives us the opportunity to consider the many proposals and the most influential evidence, cultural and social, where professionals need to learn about opportunities that their countertransference offers in a culture-based practice.

– Prof. Alejandro Ávila, PhD, Complutense University, Madrid
Training member and honorary president of
the Institute of Relational Psychotherapy
and chair of IARPP's Spanish chapter

Neil Altman's words flow with ease and grace as the book acquires a vibrancy nourished by real life illustrations of an involved psychoanalyst. The distinction of this extremely important and timely work lies in its ability to make us sit up and question the social injustice which inheres in the practice of mental health including that of psychoanalysis, psychiatry and all modern visions of managed cure. By invoking the need for community work and a reflexive cultural sensitivity, he urges his colleagues to attend to the emotional needs of those relegated to invisible social peripheries. In times of rising capitalism and increasing globalisation, Neil Altman thus speaks to us from the depths of an awakened conscience and emerges as a unique voice, committed to humanising an engaged and relational psychotherapeutic-psychoanalytical approach.

– Honey Oberoi Vahali, Dean, School of Human Studies and
Director, Centre of Psychotherapy and Clinical Research,
Ambedkar University Delhi, India

# Psychoanalysis in an Age of Accelerating Cultural Change

## Spiritual Globalization

Neil Altman

Routledge
Taylor & Francis Group

LONDON AND NEW YORK

First published 2015
by Routledge
27 Church Road, Hove, East Sussex, BN3 2FA

And by Routledge
711 Third Avenue, New York, NY 10017

*Routledge is an imprint of the Taylor & Francis Group,*
*an informa business*

*British Library Cataloguing in Publication Data*
A catalogue record for this book is available from the British
Library

*Library of Congress Cataloging-in-Publication Data*
Altman, Neil, 1946– , author.
   Psychoanalysis in an age of accelerating cultural change :
spiritual globalization / Neil Altman.
      p. ; cm.
   Includes bibliographical references.
   I. Title.
[DNLM: I. Psychoanalysis. 2. Community Mental Health
Services. 3. Cultural Characteristics. 4. Internationality.
5. Social Change. WM 460]
   RC506
   616.89'17—dc23
   2014038108

ISBN: 978-0-415-81255-9 (hbk)
ISBN: 978-0-415-81256-6 (pbk)
ISBN: 978-1-315-71933-7 (ebk)

Typeset in Times New Roman
by Apex CoVantage, LLC

For Jillian

# Contents

# Preface

Donnel Stern (2002) once commented: "We know no more about where our ordinary, unremarkable, reflective experience comes from than we do where clairvoyance or thought transmission does" (p. 516). If we don't know where our ordinary thoughts come from, how can one hope to know or explain where a book comes from?

Nonetheless, I am moved to say something about where I think this book comes from within me so that you, the reader, will understand where I am coming from in my interests and (occasionally impassioned) opinions and beliefs.

I love psychoanalysis and I am, from time to time, disappointed, if not appalled, by the way it is deployed in the world. I love the way psychoanalysis, at its best, can make us curious about our blind spots (blind spots being one form taken by the unconscious) so that we can learn from our mistakes. Not that we won't keep on making mistakes (the unconscious is ubiquitous), but we can hope to keep on learning from them. I was delighted when contemporary psychoanalysis, especially relational versions, opened up the social world for psychoanalytic investigation, while making psychotherapeutic technique more flexible so that one could envision doing psychoanalytic therapy in the public sector. In the tradition of Isaiah Berlin, who taught us that there is no set of values that transcends conflict and choice, Stephen Mitchell taught me and us that there is no psychoanalytic theory or practice beyond personal commitment and choice in the face of uncertainty.

I love diversity among people. I love learning new things about cultures. When I travel, I prefer to sit in cafes, or ride in the metro, watching and listening to people and trying to get a feel for what life is like for them. I lived in a small village in India for nearly three years, have taught in Delhi for a number of years, and have travelled extensively around the world; I'm eager to see new places and meet new people.

Put all this together, and you can understand how I would seek to use psychoanalysis to raise my consciousness as best I can, to learn about my own prejudices and ethnocentrism and to observe how I, and my colleagues, recoil from the suffering of others. I attempt to see into my blind spots in my clinical work (in collaboration with my patients) and in the world at large (with my friends and others).

I like to get out into the world as a clinician and to address human suffering where people live; I am drawn to community-based work. I worked in public clinics in the Bronx and at Head Start in Newark for a number of years and would not have had it otherwise. I like office-based work as well, but find the office, to a degree, an artificial environment. It's certainly the therapist's turf.

I am appalled by psychoanalytic elitism and isolation. I want to use the psychoanalytic method of investigation of anxiety and defense to challenge my field, and myself, to live up to our own ideals of self-awareness, of learning from experience, especially from our failures, and to seek awareness of how we avoid suffering, shame, guilt, and pain at the expense of our humanity.

That's where I'm coming from, as best I can tell you. I hope that puts my biases and passions on the table so that we can begin a conversation.

# Acknowledgments

This book was conceived in a conversation with Jillian Stile, then soon to be my wife, in a Punjabi restaurant in New Delhi. We were sharing some new ideas. "You should write another book." That's how life renews.

Then there was Ashok Nagpal's office in the School of Human Studies at Ambedkar University in Delhi. This was the incubator. Sitting with faculty: Rachana Johri, Honey Vahali, sometimes Anup Dhar and Shyam Menon. There was always homemade food to share, warmth, community. A home from which to start and a rare commitment to human welfare and humanity combined with subtle intelligence.

Rico Ainslie and Daphny Ainslie, you are my inspiration in so many ways. Rico, you are my model for an engaged psychoanalyst.

Also home has been my twenty-three-year-old Friday study group in New York: Sabrina Wolfe, Cassandra Cook, Sarah Hahn Burke, and Richard Fulmer. You were and are always there with challenge, support, and deep understanding. Thank you. Thank you to Cleonie White for the opportunity to learn from you as we teach together.

And thanks to David Ramirez in Philadelphia, Alejandro Avila Espada in Madrid, and Frederico Periera and Miguel Moita in Lisbon for your invitations. You don't know how much they meant to me.

Larry Siegel and Bob Levine, you are my rocks of Gibraltar through thick and thin.

Kate Hawes and Lewis Aron fortify me with their support and confidence in the idea for this book.

And, always, Jillian: you find a way to make beauty in all circumstances, from rickshaws in Delhi to Central Park West. That's how life is sustained.

# Chapter 1

# Introduction

## Psychoanalysis, Community-Based Clinical Work, Culture

In writing this book, my starting point is my unease about social injustice in the world of psychotherapy and mental health services more generally. Those who are materially privileged, especially in the United States, have access to careful, thorough attention to the origin and resolution of their psychological distress through psychoanalytically informed therapy. By and large, people who are materially disadvantaged have access only to time-limited, narrowly goal-oriented, and cost efficiency-focused psychotherapy and medication-based treatments. In the private sector, people can choose the form of treatment or intervention they wish and find useful and fulfilling. In the public sector, people's choices take a back seat to whatever promises to save money for governments in the short run. At the present budget and tax-cutting moment, government-funded mental health services are focused on saving money in all health-related areas. The integration of "behavioral health" (as mental health is now termed), with general health, entails a focus on higher rates of obesity leading to diabetes and heart disease and asthma among mentally ill people. Behavioral change leading to weight loss and to compliance with treatment for diabetes, in particular, is now a favored goal of public sector-funded psychological treatments. Governments want to save money and insurance companies and drug companies want profits for their shareholders; these factors affect the way psychological services are provided in both the private and public sectors around the world. As a reputedly cost-ineffective form of treatment, anything smacking of psychoanalysis seems out of step with the times.

Meanwhile, psychoanalysis as a field has colluded with its own marginalization by an inattention to—and a splendid isolation from—the material concerns of the larger society. Private practice-based, psychoanalytically informed psychotherapy survives, if not thrives, where there are high levels of income inequality. Those practitioners who have access to the materially privileged few can do the careful, thorough work of psychoanalytic exploration. For those with successful private practices, there is no material inducement to challenge this situation; on the contrary, there is a vested interest in maintaining the status quo. Those who practice with the less materially privileged live and work in a different world of public budget cuts and insurance company oversight that seems inimical to the ethos of psychoanalysis. A practice that, in theory, honors the humanity of people ends up in danger of dehumanizing, by inattention and marginalization, the great majority. Over time, it comes to seem only natural that psychoanalytic therapy is meant for the economically privileged with their educational attainments and value systems. It comes to seem only natural that the economically and educationally disadvantaged lack whatever it takes to benefit from psychoanalytic therapy, even if they could afford it. What gets lost when these conclusions are taken for granted is the notion that psychoanalytically cultivated attention to feelings in the context of relationships could be at least as important to those who can only be reached in the public sector. Practitioners risk getting emotionally overwhelmed and burnt out when they leave the relative comfort of the private office to engage the suffering of the economically disadvantaged in the communities where they can be reached. What if clinicians who work in the public sector, or with the less materially advantaged in the private sector, need the psychoanalytic orientation to process feelings, their own and those of their patients, as much as clinicians working in private offices? That question is the starting point of this book.

At this point, a word about what I mean by "psychoanalysis" is in order. Freud (1914) said that any method of treatment that focused on transference and resistance could call itself psychoanalysis. Elsewhere, he defined psychoanalysis as the science of unconscious mental processes (Freud, 1925). In the sense in which I am using the word in this book, psychoanalysis is a theory and technique that focuses on the unconscious aspects of the emotional relationship between patient and therapist. In other language, the psychoanalytic method is directed toward drawing out and exploring the patient's meaning-making systems, especially as they are manifest in the patient-therapist relationship. Freud prescribed, as do some of today's classically oriented practitioners, a particular frame for doing this work, e.g. the couch, multiple meetings per week, a neutral, anonymous stance in relation to the patient. This frame has been called into question more recently by other analysts, as will be discussed below; I regard these "technical" prescriptions as secondary. Specific technical practices have cultural and personal meanings that themselves must be explored in a psychoanalytic therapy. Flexibility in technique in the service of establishing a psychoanalytic relationship is key to reaching a wide range of people across cultural and socioeconomic groups. But the principle of helping people develop increased awareness and understanding of themselves and their interactions with others remains. Consciousness-raising with respect to self and others is itself a goal with cultural and personal meanings. Self-awareness is not for everyone; self-awareness may be discouraged or considered irrelevant in some cultural contexts. Everyone has some conflict about the degree to which they *want* to know themselves and significant others. Psychoanalysis does not transcend culture any more than any other discipline or practice. What saves psychoanalysis from being simply partisan with respect to the value of awareness of self and others is that the field and its practitioners are enjoined to be self-reflective about its values and commitments.

So, this book is about psychoanalysis, about community mental health work, and about culture. All three. And necessarily so. I suggest that one thinks best about any of these subjects in the context of the other two. I further suggest that each of these fields benefits from a degree of integration with the other two. A key aim of this book is to demonstrate the validity of this proposition.

Psychoanalysis, community-based clinical work, cultural studies. Each of these fields tends toward constructing a world of its own with a distinctive, often insular, point of view. In a sense, each field constitutes a culture of its own—with its own language and concepts and practices—based on the job it is trying to do, what it is trying to understand, and the context in which it operates. Psychoanalysts are trying to unearth hidden meanings and patterns. Many, as noted, tend to think that they require a fairly controlled and standardized environment in which to study the interactions with and communications from their patients.

Community-based clinicians tend to have little control over the environments in which they work. They are usually confronted with communities in economic poverty that are subjected to various forms of oppression and discrimination. They tend to work with large numbers of patients with relatively severe psychological problems, along with problems of socioeconomic origin. There is a premium on symptom relief, on surviving the crush of patients in crisis, on survival. Community-based clinical workers tend to see the intensive rigorous work of psychoanalysts as a luxury not feasible in the environments in which they work. Psychoanalysts tend to think of community-based workers as doing necessary and admirable work that is not analytic because the environment is too chaotic, the patients too challenged with nonpsychologically based problems, and perhaps too besieged to introspect in the analytically required way.

Culture is a primary focus for some clinicians and theoreticians. In academia, cultural studies tend to draw on psychoanalysis, along with other fields, to explore hidden or obscure meanings in cultural productions, including popular culture. These theorists may be interested in the cultural dynamics of oppression and denigration.

Community-based clinicians may focus on culture for pragmatic reasons: their clientele, as well as the clinicians themselves, have always been culturally diverse. Community-based clinicians focus on culture to more easily form an alliance and to understand their patients.

In an effort to bring together psychoanalysis, cultural studies, and community-based clinical work, we will look backward and forward and outward. Backward in time to ponder how these three fields came to be as disconnected as they are. We will review some of the ways in which narratives of spirit possession, the summoning of spirits, and exorcism were transformed under the influence of the European Enlightenment. At the core of the Enlightenment was a splitting, a parting of the ways, between religion, faith, and spirituality on one side, and science and reason on the other. We track how the narratives of psychoanalysis moved away from spirit possession as the field evolved from a religious framework to a scientific one in the understanding and treatment of what contemporary people now call "mental illness." The disavowal of religion and faith in favor of science and reason is by no means total, however. We consider how overcoming this split and reclaiming some of the spiritual sensibility can reunite psychoanalysis with people around the world who otherwise turn only to spiritual healers of various sorts when they suffer. The Enlightenment-bred split between reason and faith or emotion is a cultural phenomenon. When reason is placed in the superior position, the stage is set for many forms of prejudice and colonial domination, as we will see.

We look forward to speculate about where some of the trends often referred to as "globalization" appear to be taking us. Globalization refers to the ascendance of free market capitalism all around the world. Faith in free markets, and I use the term "faith" advisedly, has resulted in the rise of competitive values globally (another cultural phenomenon). Free market ideology also leads to the enforced shrinking of the public sector that supports mental health services for economically disadvantaged people at the very time that they need it most (i.e., when many of them find themselves uprooted from traditional ways of living and traditional ways of making a living). We will reflect on the ways in which mental health services are evolving and changing in response to the ever-increasing pressure to do more with less.

Finally, we will look outward to various parts of the world to learn about cultural differences and about how people are responding to globalization. We will focus especially carefully on the United States and India, where I have had the most experience, as well as on Portugal and other parts of Europe and Asia. We will note, for example, that there has not been the same kind of split between science and spirituality in India that occurred in Europe. Comparing how psychoanalysis and public sector mental health services have evolved in the United States and in India, for example, can expand the horizons of all involved about the impact their particular cultural situation has had on their own theories and practices. We will consider how people in India and Europe, to take another example, resist global capitalism in a way that is relatively rare in the United States, with consequences in how people feel about, and respond to, their shrinking public sector.

This book is not a textbook in psychoanalysis or public sector mental health nor in global capitalism. I do not attempt a comprehensive look at any of these fields. A degree of familiarity with psychoanalysis and public sector mental health services is assumed, though I aim to present my ideas in an accessible form that will speak to a wide range of readers. My sensibility throughout is nonlinear and contextual, particularly with respect to culture and personality. If you wonder what exactly I mean by that, please read on.

# Chapter 2

# Psychoanalysis and Culture

Psychoanalysts may gravitate toward an interest in culture as a source of uncon-scious structuring of the mind. Freud (2002) believed that culture itself had psycho-logical origins in the dynamics of superego formation. Layton (2006) coined the term "normative unconscious" to refer to the way in which culturally conditioned norms operate outside of awareness to mold feelings, attitudes, and behavior. I have referred to cultures as worlds of meaning that exist largely out of conscious awareness (Altman, 2010). Nonetheless, psychoanalysts have, until quite recently, largely ignored culture, seeing it as a sociological factor that is extra-analytic. Psychoanalytic patients and practitioners tend to be quite homogenous culturally. With cultural diversity on the rise in the countries where analysts function, it has begun to be recognized that effective analytic work requires an understanding of the interaction of cultural worlds of meaning between patient and analyst. The relational turn in psychoanalysis has facilitated the recognition that one cannot so easily separate the inner, intrapsychic world from the cultural worlds of meaning in which people are socialized.

As a psychoanalyst who has worked cross-culturally, I have been impressed with the serviceability of psychoanalysis in contemporary contexts of cultural flux. With Indian patients, for example, I have noted that psychoanalytic introspec-tion seems to open up and enrich private mental space for people whose culture is evolving to add an individual dimension to a traditional focus on community. Psychoanalytic introspection, in particular, opens up an individual, private space filled with myth and the unknown—qualities that often speak to an Indian sen-sibility. Psychoanalysis, with its focus on the unconscious (or, as I prefer to say, unconsciousness, or better, unknowability) has a way of straddling fences, speak-ing to both sides of a contradiction, and generating paradoxes. In other words, psychoanalysis provides a place for self-exploration for those who are in the midst of cultural shifts, conflicts, and contradictions (i.e., all of us these days, but some of us more obviously than others). Psychoanalysis also contains enough undefined space to leave room for various cultural groups to fill in the gaps with their own material and sensibility. This very quality, however, leaves psychoanalysis open to co-optation by cultural forces that may militate against its inclusiveness. In the United States, as we will see, psychoanalysis and psychoanalysts have found a place for themselves in a competitive, capitalist context that yields materialism and a high degree of economic inequality. Psychoanalysis has become a treatment for the well-to-do in a way that reduces, but does not eliminate, its intercultural location.

As a function of having addressed very different socioeconomic groups in the United States, psychoanalysts and community-based clinicians live in largely different worlds, speak different languages, and have different agendas. Each of these different worlds needs an integration or accommodation with the other in order to advance our understanding of human beings and to work with people productively. Community-based workers would benefit from the understanding of transference, countertransference, and the unconscious that psychoanalysis provides. Psychoanalysts would likewise benefit from the contact with the real world and the perspectives found in community-based clinical work on how race, social class, and culture shape people. Community-based workers are familiar with how being underprivileged shapes people. Psychoanalysts may be much less familiar with how *privilege* shapes people. Community-based workers are familiar with how experience as a member of a discriminated-against racial or ethnic group shapes people. Psychoanalysts may be less familiar with how the experience of discriminating against others may shape people. Bringing the perspectives of psychoanalysis and of community-based clinical work together will help community-based workers perform their jobs, and it will help analysts note and work with the blind spots around the shaping influence of being white, of being affluent, and of being culturally mainstream that comes with being insulated. The challenge in this book is to find a middle ground that is neither psychoanalytic-centric, nor symptom management-centric, nor cultural-centric. I seek to be "multicultural" in the sense that immigrants or other people who travel between worlds can have a rich perspective on each. I tack back and forth between psychoanalytic, community, and cultural points of view in the interest of putting all three perspectives into play. In that spirit, I now examine these three perspectives in interaction, hoping to keep all of them in mind as we proceed.

## Psychoanalysis Suffers from Elitism and Isolation

Psychoanalysis is commonly thought to be an office-based practice. This preconception derives from both theoretical and socioeconomic factors: there is the idea that the analysis of transference, at the core of psychoanalysis, can only be carried out when the analyst is anonymous, when his personality is not exposed, and when he is neutral in the sense of not taking sides in the patient's conflicts. Classically, being neutral entails restricting one's interventions to objective interpretations. From this classical point of view, the patient's internal, psychological reality can only come into focus when external reality, including the reality of the analyst's personality, can be factored out. The private office offers a protected, standardized environment in which anonymity and neutrality can be preserved. Public clinics and community-based venues, like the patient's home or a nearby diner or park bench, expose the patient to all sorts of random and unforeseen eventualities that threaten to compromise confidentiality and the analyst's professional composure. Too much can happen that the analyst must handle spontaneously. Contemporary, relationally oriented analysts, however, have come to believe that anonymity and neutrality are impossible in principle. According to this view, everything the analyst does exposes her personality, including any effort she might make to be anonymous. All interpretations are also actions in the sense that they express and convey the analyst's personal and subjective experience of the patient, not simply objectively derived information. The community-based venue, while certainly less controlled than the private office in some ways, is not qualitatively different from the private office. The patient's internal reality and the context created by external reality, including the analyst's participation, constantly interact. It is not impossible, in principle, to carry out the analysis of transference, or countertransference in a public clinic or in a community-based environment.

When the European analysts, fleeing the Nazis, relocated to North America, they found a comfortable and secure niche for themselves in the medical model/ private practice system that was dominant, then, as now, in the United States. Thus located, psychoanalysis came to serve a largely white, affluent clientele. In the process, psychoanalysis became culturally and socioeconomically limited in terms of clientele and background of the analysts themselves. Psychoanalysis came to be seen as less than relevant to people from nonmainstream cultural backgrounds, from lower or even middle socioeconomic status, and to those who were beset by poverty, prejudice, or other socioeconomic problems. Psychoanalysis removed itself, to a significant extent, from the social world.

The pre-World War II analysts of Europe, however, had made serious efforts to make psychoanalytic therapy available to people of limited means, as Elizabeth Danto (2005) documented in *Freud's Free Clinics*. In the United States, some analytically trained or inclined practitioners were always working in schools, hospitals, or public sector clinics. To one degree or another, they used analytic concepts in processing their clinical experiences in these settings. In the analytic community, however, and in society at large, this sort of clinical work was not seen as essentially analytic. A distinction was made between psychoanalysis, carried out under conditions of anonymity and neutrality in a strictly regulated frame, and psychotherapy, which was adaptable to the less-than-ideal conditions obtaining out in the world. Psychoanalysis was seen as the elite treatment for the elite of society, in contrast to psychotherapy for those who did not have the time or the money for the "pure gold" (Freud, 1919).

As societies become more culturally diverse all over the world, and as the reputation of psychoanalysis has suffered among mental health practitioners and the public at large, analysts are seeking to expand the cultural and socioeconomic applicability of their theory and practice. This book seeks to demonstrate that taking psychoanalysis out into the world can enrich and expand the field, making it more culturally aware and sensitive, and making it more appealing to more practitioners in more settings and to more potential recipients of mental health services. The focus on the isolated individual of the medical-model-derived form psychoanalysis has taken, especially in the United States, does not speak to many people around the world. For example, in many cultural contexts, what Western workers with a medical model might refer to as "psychopathology" is seen as a community event in the sense that the cause as well as the cure for the symptomatic behavior might be thought to lie out in the community. Holmes (2012) noted this way of looking at symptomatic behavior as he worked at a drop-in clinic in Lima, Peru. Symptomatic behavior thought to reflect spirit possession in India is often seen as caused by an envious attack by family members or others in the community. A curse might be placed on one member of a family, but be taken up by another member of the family as part of a gender-related responsibility or role (Pfleiderer, 2006). Therapeutic responsibility is often assigned to family members in India (Kakar, 1982) and in Africa (Bührmann, 1984). Maiello (1999) noted such community involvement in her conversations with a traditional healer in South Africa. Maiello, citing Buhrmann (1984), notes that "the question asked in African culture is not *what* caused illness, but *who* brought it about" (p. 227). She also writes, "the therapeutic system is composed not only of a therapist and a patient with the conscious and unconscious parts of their personalities, but comprises, on the one side the healer including his or her ancestors, and, on the other, the patient, including both his clan and his ancestors" (p. 227). In South Africa, she found that symptoms were often thought to reflect unfinished business with ancestors. The cure often involved the healing of relationships with ancestors that had been neglected, bringing in a trans-generational element and a sense of internal ancestors that line up well with the object relations theory of the West. In short, in many cultural contexts, healing cannot occur without community involvement, including the family, the clan, and sometimes, ancestors. Kiev (1972) wrote,

> the Freudian model, which attributes behavior primarily to internal, psychic motivations, derives as much from Western culture as it does from the objective study of behavior. It does not pay as much attention, however, to the social determinants of behavior as the pre-scientific model does in certain traditional cultures, in which the individual is believed to act in relationship to his ancestors, the community, and the opinions and expectations of others.
>
> (p. 18)

Note how Kiev, in this passage, though he is trying to make room for cultural context in the understanding of behavior, places "traditional" cultural understandings in an inferior, relatively undeveloped position as "prescientific." This point aside, he suggests that if therapists are to reach people whose cultural way of understanding is "traditional," in the sense that he uses the word, a place must be made for the role of the community, including prior generations of people. If psychoanalysis is to go out into the world, including people whose cultural framework is "traditional," it must accommodate a more communal, trans-generational understanding into its framework. From a perspective nearly forty years after Kiev, we see that psychoanalytic theory has indeed become more open to social perspectives. A place can be made in psychoanalysis for the role of ancestors in people's lives via the psychoanalytic concept of "internal objects." If psychoanalysis is to expand more broadly into the community, it must be as a theory and practice that sees individuals and communities as completely intertwined. Contemporary developments in psychoanalysis, initiated by analysts such as Winnicott and Harry Stack Sullivan, have been directed toward elaborating on the interpersonal context of the individual's psychic life. Consideration of the larger social and cultural context of psychic life has been developed by a range of analysts, including Kakar (1982, 2008), Layton (2006), and many others.

Here's the rub: in the wake of colonialism and capitalism, individualistic values are regarded as more evolved and mature than communal values. Psychoanalysis, and psychoanalysts in a search for prestige, has identified itself with the value system that carries prestige in Western cultures. If one believes that psychoanalysis is defined by its individual focus, it may indeed be the case that it cannot speak to the majority of people, especially those from more communal cultures. But if one thinks of psychoanalysis as, instead, defined by focus on unconscious aspects of transference and countertransference, there is no reason why it cannot encompass a variety of understandings of symptomatic behavior that take account of the surrounding community as well as trans-generational processes. By holding to a self-definition as exclusive, the gold standard, elite, and by and for the economically privileged, prestige is purchased at the cost of the ability to address the suffering of most of humanity. If psychoanalysis is about challenging our defenses against the awareness of suffering, then psychoanalytic values would lead us to seek to become aware of, and to challenge, this pursuit of privilege and the dehumanization of self and others that goes with it.

## The Cultural Location of Psychoanalysis Reflects the Cultures of Psychoanalysts

Sigmund Freud was an Eastern European Jew living in Vienna during the late nineteenth and early-to-mid-twentieth centuries. He was one of the first Jews allowed to attend medical school, and later to treat non-Jewish patients. Freud was thus concerned that psychoanalysis not be pigeon-holed as a "Jewish Science." He presented his theory as universal, including his developmental framework, theory of health and pathology, and of pathogenesis (Aron & Starr, 2012; Gay, 1987; Gilman, 1993).

Given that Freud was a Jew who was heavily influenced by Northern and Eastern European cultures, it is not surprising that we find Jewish and Northern European cultural elements in the culture of psychoanalysis. Among the elements that seem recognizably, though not exclusively, Jewish is the Talmudic-style interpretive approach to the patients' productions as texts. The premium on words also seems to be clearly in the Jewish tradition. In a broader sense, Freud (1925) himself referred to the outsider status of Jews in Europe as a facilitating factor in his "independence of judgment" (i.e., his ability to critique the sexual norms of his time and place in order to expose the impulses underlying a superficial propriety). Among the recognizable, though not exclusively, Northern European elements, one might cite the emphasis on frustration, renunciation, restraint, and abstention from action.

Marie Hoffman (2010) considers how the Christian backgrounds of Winnicott, Fairbairn, and Guntrip might have influenced their particular versions of psychoanalytic theory and practice. She also finds the footprints of Christian theology and philosophy in the psychoanalytic tradition. She constructs a translation, as it were, of psychoanalytic narratives into parallel Jewish and Christian narratives, finding correspondences between key features of psychoanalysis and the prominent narratives in each religious tradition. She notes influences of Jewish and Christian narratives in the development of important psychoanalytic theorists. With respect to Christianity, in particular, Hoffman finds elements of incarnation, crucifixion, and resurrection in both psychoanalysis and Hegel's (1977, 2006) version of Christianity. In Hoffman's (2010) account, a parallel to the incarnation of God as human in Christian narrative occurs when the analyst allows himself to identify with and be transformed into the patient's internal objects, or important figures from the patient's past and present life. Incarnation is followed by crucifixion as the analyst, thus transformed into the people who had in the past failed or had a destructive impact on the patient, is attacked. In a successful analysis, this attack, or fantasied destruction, is survived by the analyst, leading to resurrection. The parallel here is between the crucifixion and resurrection of Christ and Winnicott's (1969) idea of object usage. In each case, a new form of life and intersubjectivity emerges from survival of a real (or fantasied) death.

Hindu/Buddhist sensibilities can be discerned in some elements of psychoanalytic theory and technique, though the pathways of influence are sometimes obscure. Emmanual Ghent (1990, 1992), Jeremy Safran (2003), and a number of other authors have been explicit about being influenced by Eastern religious thought and practice. These analysts have noted how meditation—in particular, being deeply introspective—has much in common with the free associative spirit of acceptance of whatever comes to mind. Ghent (1990, 1992) has elucidated brilliantly the parallel between the Hindu/Buddhist notion of "ego" (the meaning of which is more like the self in a narcissistic sense than the psychoanalytic notion of the ego as a functional aspect of the self) and the Winnicottian-psychoanalytic "false self." Following Ghent, from either an Eastern religious or a psychoanalytic perspective, resistance is not to be opposed. Resistance is to be noted, whether in meditation or free association, in which case it may melt away. Morita therapy (Doi, 1962; Kiev, 1972; Morita, 1998) likewise aims at developing acceptance of symptoms and anxiety, rather than efforts to eliminate them. In the Zen tradition of Japan, as in the Hindu/Buddhist traditions of India and elsewhere in Asia, the goal is to let thoughts and feelings, of whatever sort, arise and pass away like clouds in the sky (even massive storms). In the paradoxical vision of these traditions, the effort to let go of anxiety or depression or resistance to the process of whatever sort only strengthens that which is opposed, much like how insomnia is made more severe by trying to fall asleep. The fundamental problem is attachment to, or investment in, a particular outcome or self-state. But attachment or investment in itself is to be noted and allowed to be, and to pass. Homa Morita (1998), the founder of Morita therapy, further believed that anxiety and depression resulted from "useless self observation" (p. 28) (i.e., self-observation that breaks the harmony between person and experience and that interrupts the spontaneity or flow of experience). In that sense, the path of Zen Buddhist meditation is mindfulness, not in the sense of standing aside and observing experience, but rather in being at one with experience. In this way, the self-observing function of the psychoanalytic ego is perhaps at odds, in a subtle way, with the Eastern meditative tradition. The Morita/Zen approach also discourages trying to make the mind focus on one point, idea, or image. Anxiety is thought to result from overly focused attention so that the mind is not free to move about in a natural way. Such freedom to move would undermine the obsessive rumination of depressive or phobic anxiety.

## The Significance of Locating Psychoanalysis Culturally

Being reflective about the cultural location of psychoanalysis can sensitize us, in general, to the meanings that technical practices may have in various cultural contexts. More specifically, there may be elements in psychoanalytic technique that interfere with the building of a working alliance or with the analytic process. Notwithstanding individual differences in this regard, the classical analyst's reserve and restraint may more likely be experienced as withholding and depriving by someone from a culture that is accustomed to, or values, a high degree of relational involvement in general, or specifically with authorities (see Kakar, 1982 for a discussion of this point in an Indian context).

Awareness of cultural context may also attune us to inadvertently prejudicial elements in psychoanalytic theory. Brickman (2003), for example, points out the origin of the concept "primitive" in rationales for European colonial exploitation of people in Asia, Africa, and Latin America. Taking a concept with origins in the Catholic Church's way of referring to nonbelievers, apologists for colonialism referred to colonized people as "primitive" (i.e., needing to be civilized). Brickman points out that the concept was then incorporated in psychoanalytic theory to refer to the id, as when Freud referred to the id as analogous to an "aboriginal population in the mind" (the title of Brickman's book, the words taken from Freud, 1915, p. 195). Brickman (2003) suggests that the prejudicial stereotype of Asian, African, and Latin American people as sexual, aggressive, irrational, and emotional is built into psychoanalytic theory in the form of an id conceived as more primitive and less mature than the rational ego. Abstention from action and an emphasis on verbalization in the context of abstinence are technical principles that derive from this theoretical perspective. Colonialism, sexism, and racism each draw from the same set of prejudices. So, it would not be surprising to find that women and people of Asian, African, and Latin American origin would find something off-putting about psychoanalytic theory and the technique that is derived from it.

## Culture in Psychoanalytic Clinical Work

This point brings us to a consideration of culture in the psychoanalytic clinical situation. I see culture as completely embedded in transference and countertransference. By that I mean that cultures, far from being a limited set of behaviors, customs, traditions, or habits, are most fundamentally meaning-systems. Customs, traditions, and so on (don't wear your shoes indoors, don't eat with your left hand, say please and thank you) are the tip of an iceberg of all-encompassing, meaning-generating systems. Not wearing your shoes indoors or not eating with your left hand in India refers to meanings around purity and pollution that are wide ranging. To begin to talk about purity and pollution will soon lead to the caste system, to the idea of karma, to the nature of self, and so on. Saying please and thank you will lead to attitudes toward need and greed and gratitude and their regulation in interpersonal situations. One thing leads to another and before you know it, you're talking about a comprehensive view of the world. That is culture: a world of meaning to live in. We tend to call the worlds of meaning that are widespread "cultural," while other worlds of meaning are more limited to the family, or to an individual. Shared worlds of meaning, i.e. cultures, are transmitted through the family; each family puts a unique spin on that cultural world of meaning depending on socially generated factors like the family's assigned race and social class. Another type of spin is generated by the unique family history: immigration, trauma, the legacy of past relationships, and so on. Of course, each individual takes in the culture through the lens of her particular personality. All of these systems of meanings, those widely shared, those family-based, and those more individually based, are intertwined. They can be considered separately for purposes of discussion, but in the end, they are impossible to separate out from each other.

Personal meaning-making systems are also very close to what psychoanalysts mean by "transference" and "countertransference." The only distinction to be made is that these latter terms refer to meaning-making systems as they emerge and are generated by the psychoanalytic situation. Psychoanalysts tend to assume that the meaning-systems that emerge in psychoanalysis are relevant to the dysfunctional meaning-systems that brought the person to seek help. The exploration and explication of meaning-making systems is the fundamental psychoanalytic task. It is not only the particular meanings that emerge in an analytic relationship that constitutes the fruit of a psychoanalytic journey, but also the process of exploring and explicating how one makes meaning in general that the analysand, and, yes, the analyst, can take away.

The exploration of meaning as it is generated between any two people, including analyst and analysand, entails a degree of exploration beyond the horizon of one's own world of meaning. Gadamer (1975) depicts each of us as living in a clearing of meaning, surrounded by a vast, even infinite, forest beyond what our particular culture or familial or individual meaning system can bring to light. Each person's horizon of understanding is limited. Any interaction between two or more people where they seek to understand each other, or even listen to each other, requires each to see beyond her own horizon of meaning. Gadamer calls this process a "fusion of horizons," where the effort to understand another person's  system of meaning results in one's own horizon being stretched. In the microcosm of a dyad, psychoanalytic or otherwise, this process entails seeing oneself through the other person's eyes. In the end, every interaction is, in part, a cross-cultural journey. Cross-cultural work in psychotherapy and psychoanalysis is continuous with all the other therapeutic work that we do.

Given that the psychoanalytic concepts of unconscious transference and countertransference can be so illuminating about cross-cultural interactions, it is striking that the psychoanalytic literature is so limited in writing about cross-cultural clinical work. The reason for this is twofold: traditionally, culture was considered to lie outside the domain of psychoanalysis, defined as the intrapsychic. Culture belonged to sociology, anthropology, and social psychology. At most, psychoanalysts might allow that internal objects have a cultural flavor, or that a cultural factor might interfere with analytic work, or that there are distinctly cultural patterns of drive and defense. In all of these cases, however, culture was reduced to its shaping effect on the internal world. With the advent of two-person, relational psychologies in psychoanalysis, there appeared more space to consider the social world, in the form of other people, as lying within the domain of psychoanalysis. It remained for three-person psychologies (Altman, 2010; Lacan, 1972) to make room for contextual forces, such as social structure, language, and meaning systems, as they shape the individual and interpersonal relationships.

A second reason that psychoanalysts have paid little attention to culture derives from the presumption that most psychoanalytic practices are relatively homogenous culturally. This presumption is actually false, however. Even in cases where analyst and analysand have nominally the same cultural location, there are culturally derived differences that may be obscure and unexplored unless they are inquired into and examined.

I have taught courses on race, class, and culture to psychoanalytic candidates and graduates on many occasions. Often, the students seem quite homogeneously European or Euro-American ethnically and culturally. I typically devote as much time as I can to "cultural/ethnic introductions" in which each student or candidate describes his cultural and ethnic background. Even in cases where people have been together as a class for three or four years, they learn fascinating aspects of each other's backgrounds that they had never known. For example, who has an African American, or a Native American, or a Latin American ancestor? Whose grandparents were mixed ethnically, a Jew marrying an Italian, an Italian marrying an Irish person? Whose ancestors were survivors of the Jewish or Armenian holocaust? What family turmoil or rifts resulted from an intermarriage? And so on and so on. If psychoanalytic candidates are not discussing such things in the entire course of their training, it is not to be expected that their antennae will be out for such factors as they get to know their patients.

# Chapter 3

# Psychoanalysis and Community-Based Clinical Work

## Some Background about Community-Based Clinical Work

Community-based clinical work takes place in two contexts: the public, or governmental, sector and the nonprofit or nongovernmental sector composed of nongovernmental organizations (NGOs), known in the United States as nonprofit corporations. In both of these contexts, a balance must be struck between funding pressures and minimization of cost on one side, and the mission of the organization (i.e., to attend to psychological problems or mental illness) on the other.

In the United States, the 1960s saw relatively generous government funding of mental health in the form of the Community Mental Health Act of 1963. A central motivation was to save money. People with serious and persistent mental illness were being hospitalized, sometimes for long periods, at great public expense. The idea was to "de-institutionalize," that is, to shut down as many of the mental hospitals, or at least wards, as possible and release the patients for community-based treatment. Toward that end, federally funded community mental health centers were to provide various levels of outpatient and partial hospitalization treatment to allow mentally ill people to live in the community, to have treatment available in the community, and to have follow-up to make sure they were receiving that care.

Federal funding was to phase out after eight years, with the states and municipalities gradually to pick up the cost of the mental health centers. Many of the state and local governments did not pick up the cost, or picked up a fraction of the cost, so that services were in fact phased out through the sixties and seventies. Mentally ill people, discharged from hospitals, but not receiving community-based treatment, ended up living on the street across the United States. Many of them medicated themselves with illegal drugs; the "Rockefeller" drug laws, with mandatory minimum sentences for drug-related offenses, resulted in the mentally ill ending up in jails and prisons (Kupers, 1990). At the time of this writing, the cost of maintaining prisons has skyrocketed so that states are trying to move some inmates back into the community. In California, this form of "community-based corrections" entailed downsizing parole for which the state pays, while moving released inmates to probation, which is a responsibility of the counties (Beth Kita, personal communication, December 29, 2013). The parole system had provided more support for former inmates, as they were required to report in to parole officers. Former inmates on probation report to probation officers, who have higher caseloads and fewer reporting responsibilities. Parole officers would often provide support to mentally or physically ill parolees by ensuring that they were making and keeping necessary appointments, while aiding them in meeting a myriad of other needs. Parole also had clinical staff on site to ensure that released inmates were seen immediately and provided with timely mental health treatment. With people who would have been on parole now instead on probation, there is much less support because probation, as its task is defined, provides less intensive community supervision. The services available to these people will now depend on what is provided by counties, varying with ability and willingness to expand their own support services for those with special needs. In anticipation of the county taking over responsibility for most released offenders, the mental health services at parole were reduced, staff was laid off, and caseloads have skyrocketed, with some parts of the state relying on telemedicine in lieu of face to face appointments with psychiatrists.

Another group of people hitting the streets are long-term offenders, who are being released as a result of a federal order to the state of California to de-crowd its prisons. Many of these people spent years in prison addressing their addictions, violent actions, and mental health issues, having earned college degrees, drug-counseling certifications, and other forms of education and training. The next round of people to be released are likely to be those who are eligible for release regardless of how much rehabilitation has occurred or how much work they have done on themselves. As the state continues to release long-term offenders, "lifers," and "three strikers," community mental health systems will be challenged to provide interventions to a population whose needs are arguably the most complex. Thus, the overwhelming burden of troubled, mentally ill, acting-out people on the reduced staff in parole departments and in county-funded mental health clinics is yet to come. The cycle that began with state hospital deinstitutionalization has resumed, but without a community mental health act this time around. There are bright spots: the county of San Francisco established a peer mentoring program for some of the newly released "lifers" on parole, while the probation department and counties will be expanding mental health services available to former inmates to the extent that they have the resources and are willing to allocate them.

As funding for community-based treatment was cut in the 1970s and onward, there were consequences for clinicians on the ground. Caseloads grew with increasing pressure to do short-term treatment while extensively documenting that treatment in terms of progress toward clearly defined goals and objectives. As the politics of the United States moved in a rightward direction, government and the public sector lost revenue, and the pressures to cut cost only increased. More overwhelmed, emotionally stressed, burned-out clinicians had to work with more disturbed patients.

The idea that costs could be cut and patients treated successfully was fed by the pharmaceutical industry. These corporations marketed the idea that drugs were a more efficient way of treating mental illness than talk therapy. Everyone would benefit; patients would be treated in an "evidence-based" way (the evidence being gathered by the pharmaceutical companies themselves, or university-based researchers often funded by the pharmaceutical companies), and the burden on taxpayers would decrease. The cost of talk therapy could be reduced too, as short-term, behavioral and cognitive-behavioral treatments were developed, buttressed by brief, psycho-educational interventions.

Evidence was produced that these short-term therapies were successful, though research must always be scrutinized for how concepts are operationalized. In the case of short-term psychotherapy, a crucial question is directed at the length of the follow-up in which the success of treatment is assessed. How is that success defined and measured? What is the rate of patient recidivism over a long term, compared to longer-term treatments? Long-term longitudinal research is rarely conducted; pharmaceutical companies do not want to delay marketing their products. University-based researchers do not want to wait to publish results as they face pressures to "publish or perish."

Cutting costs, cost benefit analysis, documentation of progress in terms of behaviorally defined goals and objectives—all this occurs at the level of administration and bureaucracy. On the ground, there are seriously and persistently mentally ill people trying to keep their heads above water, and clinicians who are supposed to be making that happen. In the United States, there are various programs to offer services to people who have, or are at risk of developing, serious and persistent mental illnesses. For example, there is the Assertive Community Treatment Program, known as ACT (Stein & Santos, 1998).

The ACT program focuses on a group of people who are at very high risk of otherwise needing inpatient or other forms of intensive treatment. ACT is intended to prevent the need for more intensive, and expensive, interventions by offering people coordinated multidisciplinary services in the communities where they live via home visits. These visits are made at any time of the day or night for as long as necessary. The program is implemented widely in the United States, with associated research that is considered by governmental and private funders to have demonstrated its clinical and cost effectiveness (Weisbrod, Test, & Stein, 1980). ACT programs have been successful in obtaining funding from federal, state, and local governments, as well as private foundations such as the Robert Woods Johnson foundation. Funding for these and other such programs serving those seriously mentally ill is facilitated by fee for service provisions in Medicaid. With governmental budget cuts in recent years, Medicaid funding has been restricted in terms of numbers of visits, reimbursement rates, and elimination of reimbursement for home visits. Despite funding cuts, hospitals and free-standing programs with ACT programs can apply for grants from a variety of sources at the same time, as on-site visits, at least, can be reimbursed by Medicaid. The Center for Medicare and Medicaid Services of the United States Federal Government has funded other community-based services to deliver mental health services in the community. In New York City, for example, the "Parachutes Program" provides "Need Adapted"

Mobile Crisis Teams to respond to personal crises in response to a telephone call. "Early Intervention Programs" are available in a number of states in the United States to respond to families where there is a risk of child abuse or neglect, or where children have developmental lags or disabilities. Early intervention specialists make home visits to provide counseling and support to parents and families.

## "Evidence Based" Manualized Treatment

The manuals used to train mental health professionals and paraprofessionals who are conducting community-based clinical work emphasize "cultural competence" and collaborative work with "stakeholders" in the community (Substance Abuse and Mental Health Services Administration, 2008). These manuals tend to emphasize the importance of research, both process research and outcome research, on the "evidence based practice" being employed. Process research with respect to a particular technique, like ACT, tends to concern the degree to which the method employed faithfully replicates the evidence-based model (McHugo, Drake, Teague, & Xie, 1999). Outcome research tends to concern the degree to which short-term and quantifiable goals and objectives have been met. The manual for ACT claims that demonstrating that the method is successful increases utilization rates by people in a particular community.

The manual cited above offers vignettes illustrating effective utilization of the ACT practice. The problem with such vignettes, from my perspective, is that the vignettes all concern successful treatment. In that respect, they do not prepare practitioners for the inevitable failures they will encounter in work with patients, not to mention how to cope with, and utilize to therapeutic ends, the psychological stress associated with work in the community. Most crucially, the manual does not suggest that therapeutic "failures" are often the means by which practitioners are inducted into the tragic and despairing lives of their clients. This is not to say that despair and failure need to be the endpoint of community-based work with people experiencing extreme suffering, or even ordinary suffering, but it must certainly be the starting point for a meaningful connection with people.

Cultural competence is a particularly problematic notion. The manual cited above acknowledges that cultural competence is difficult to come by, but attributes this problem to lack of sufficient evidence. The manual further advocates that patients be assigned to workers of similar cultural background. I agree that cultural competence is difficult to come by, but I regard the process of coming to a mutual understanding as key to the therapeutic process itself. That is, negotiating similarities and differences in systems of meaning is crucial to all forms of interpersonal relatedness, in and out of the consulting room. The problem is not lack of research, because systematic, controlled research in itself could never establish the nature of what anything means in any particular culture. Each interaction between two people entails a discovery of what the exchange means to both people whether they are from the same culture or not. For that reason, finding a therapist who matches the patient in cultural terms is both impossible and unnecessary. The manual cited above acknowledges that cultures are multidimensional and that there are large, individual differences between individuals within cultures; however, the manual fails to pursue these facts to their logical conclusion that each individual and each interaction must be understood on its own terms.

## The Psychoanalytic Notion of Countertransference Is Essential in Community-Based Work

Affect is contagious. There are parallel processes by which patterns are replicated within a system. Thus, clinicians working within overwhelmed and besieged communities end up feeling overwhelmed and besieged themselves. Defenses are activated on individual and social levels among the clinicians; these manage anxiety and trauma. Meanwhile, they have dysfunctional effects on the work itself. Following is an example that illustrates a typical pattern of anxiety related to community-based work.

A current project in the School of Human Studies at the Ambedkar University of Delhi, India aims to develop a model for training clinicians to work within marginalized communities. Some of us on the faculty felt that before we could train students to enter a community composed of people with whom we would rarely if ever have contact we should have the experience ourselves. Thus, we, along with the students, agreed to strike up a conversation with someone in a poor community that we would normally avoid, then to process the conversation in class with each other and the students.

As I was preparing to strike up such a conversation in a nearby market, I was taking a walk for exercise on a road that was in the process of being built for the Commonwealth games in Delhi in 2010. Some high-rise buildings were being constructed to house the foreigners who were soon expected, and a new road was being prepared to make those buildings accessible. Construction workers lived in tents alongside the road. Women and men were breaking stones to cover the pavement while naked infants and barely clad children sat near them. There were latrines for these canvas encampments. As I passed by one such encampment, my eye was caught by a very thin man crossing the road with a tumbler of water in his hand, clearly planning to defecate in the field across the road rather than use the latrine. This method of defecating was once the norm all across India, but now the use of latrines is far more common.

As I passed by the encampment on my way back, I saw this man again on the side of the road. He had a baby on his hip, a little girl decked out in a pretty little dress and wearing black eye liner. The man, evidently her father, was coughing with a sound such as I had never heard. Directly on the baby. Later, I thought he must have had tuberculosis.

What I want to bring into focus is that as I passed this man, some one hundred feet away, I instinctively drew even further away from him all the way to the far edge of the road. There was no way I was close enough to catch whatever he had, but nonetheless, I needed to distance myself from him.

Later, it occurred to me that my pulling away from him represented and enacted my anxiety about my forthcoming trip into a slum market. I, along with any other middle-class-and-up clinician preparing to enter a slum would be exposed to a range of diseases from which she would normally be protected and insulated. But, most of all, what seemed communicable was the suffering. How painful would it be to know that my beautiful baby girl was being exposed to the tuberculosis that I carried?

Why is psychoanalysis helpful in this situation? Psychoanalysis is about keeping an eye on the way we avoid suffering. In psychoanalytic language, this is called "resistance." Freud's genius was to consider that when it seemed that the patient was obstructing the therapy by refusing insight, denying in some way the analyst's interpretations, this obstruction might actually reflect a manifestation of transference. That is, Freud came to see that psychoanalysis was not simply a matter of the analyst conveying insight to the patient in the form of interpretations. Psychoanalysis was about the way that the pathogenic early childhood situation was re-enacted with the analyst in such a way as to block any straightforward curative measures. The analyst, in the transference, became the parent who had been the focus of the patient's pathogenic impulses and defenses. When the patient rejected the analyst's input, this could be seen as an opportunity, the emergence of negative transference. Psychoanalysis came to pursue its goal via the obstructions encountered along the way. Freud and his followers came to see that the obstructions were the way.

Freud thought that what was transferred was an investment of the other person with sexual energy, along with the anxiety this provoked, and the defenses against this anxiety. According to this viewpoint, the patient rejected the analyst's interpretations because the interaction, the relationship itself, evoked an ancient sexual bond that was conflictual, anxiety-provoking, and thus needed to be warded off.

In recent years, there has been a proliferation of alternative ideas as to the constituent elements of transference. Some analysts think that what is transferred are patterns of interpersonal interaction in reality, and/or as perceived by the patient. Other analysts think that the patient induces or provokes the analyst to behave in ways that are reminiscent of the patient's objects of early attachment so that the early interpersonal situation is actually replicated, to a degree, in the relationship with the analyst. Some analysts, particularly those who focus on the pathogenic role of trauma, understand the analytic situation as reproducing traumatic anxiety. The goal of the therapy becomes, then, not insight per se, but the ability to contain anxiety, as opposed to warding off anxiety by resort to massive and dysfunctional defenses like distortion of reality or extreme withdrawal.

Thinking about the way people avoid the negative feelings associated with traumatic anxiety or suffering becomes a way to think about my reaction to the man with the tubercular cough and his child. I moved to the far side of the road, not to avoid the tuberculosis bacillus, but to avoid the contagious effect of this man's suffering. Before one can simply plunge into community-based work in a situation where there is extreme suffering, one must come to terms with the suffering encountered in sympathy with those whom one is trying to "help." Most people stay so far away from such suffering that the question never arises. The people at the side of the road are marginalized so as to protect mainstream society from having to encounter their suffering. People in extreme poverty and pain are dehumanized and demonized by mainstream society precisely to avoid identification with them in a way that could produce unbearable pain. Those who wish to defy such dehumanization and marginalization must first come to terms with the extreme anxiety and pain their work will entail.

People willing to undertake such work can use all the support they can get from their colleagues. Instead, the funding cuts I have described above ensure that community-based clinicians will have overwhelmingly huge caseloads and piles of paperwork. Dehumanization is reflected in caseloads so large that it is difficult to find time, energy, or psychic space to do justice to the individual's experience. Dehumanization is reflected in human suffering reduced to a quantifiable entity as required by the priority given to documentation and paperwork. The clinician's suffering in resonance with that of the patient is dismissed, as time for peer support and clinical supervision is in short supply or completely missing. All this constitutes a recipe for disaster; when clinicians work with suffering people, and when they feel dehumanized, treated like money-making or money-saving machines, their patients also treated like numbers, a profound disillusionment occurs. We call this burnout.

If there is any way for community-based clinicians to survive in this situation, they must have some perspective on the ways in which the extreme pain and anxiety that are part and parcel of life in poor communities will infect those who work there. Burnout and dehumanization are defenses against unbearable pain. Recognition of this fact can allow the clinician to see that the suffering and the dehumanization go hand in hand; the defense contains, or points toward, that which it is defending against. This is how a psychoanalytic perspective can be useful to people working in nearly impossible conditions in distressed communities with minimal support.

## A Psychoanalytic Perspective Can Be Useful in Community-Based, Economic-Development Work

Psychoanalysis can also be useful to those whose work in the community is not, strictly speaking, clinical. Following is an example of psychoanalytic consultation to people doing economic-development work in rural India.

The students in a class I co-taught were working with an NGO that focused on the economic empowerment of women living in small villages. They were enrolled in Ambedkar University of Delhi's M.Phil. program in Development Practice. In their practicum placements, they were assigned to villages where there was an NGO worker whose job it was to promote women's self-help groups. The students were discussing their initial experiences in the villages to which they were assigned. I was trying to draw them out about their feelings as they first entered their villages. Some of the students were Indians who had lived all their lives in large cities such as Delhi, although going back two or three generations, they, like most or all Indians, had roots in villages. Others had lived their entire lives in villages.

One student reported a dilemma: NGO workers had been encouraging women to raise poultry as a side business. One woman, a villager, said that she would like to raise poultry, but recent rains had washed away the shed in which she had intended to keep the chickens. If only the student would give her the money to build a new shed, she would be able to proceed with the business.

The student said she did not know what to do. She knew that she should not give money to this woman, that this was not her job. She knew that if she gave money to this one woman, other women would also ask her for money. If she started giving money out of her pocket to the women, it would undermine the effort to promote self-sufficiency. Yet, the amount was trivial to this student. She could easily afford to give the money to rebuild the shed. The student felt uneasy about saying no, afraid of offending the villager. In her conversation with the village woman, the topic turned to saris that could be obtained in Delhi. With relief, the student promised to bring the woman a sari on her next visit to the village.

Many of the students in the class clearly were resonating with this student's dilemma. The feelings of uneasiness the students had about their economic privilege among economically impoverished villagers were widely shared. They easily understood how giving money would be counterproductive, and they all recognized the discomfort about appearing to be withholding resources in the eyes of the villagers. I raised the following points.

Anyone who works with economically disadvantaged people must accept that there are huge problems that they will not be able to address, much less solve. The problems that lead to rural poverty are systemic and long standing. There may be great satisfaction in helping even one or a few women start a small business, but until that is established, and sometimes even then, it may feel both to the villagers and to the workers themselves that their contribution was a drop in the bucket. In order to work usefully with these individuals, one must accept that there will be many problems they cannot solve, and that this will sometimes feel like failure, or even a willful choice to withhold, both to themselves and to the villagers. In order to perform their job, therefore, the workers must keep their guilt and unrealistic expectations in perspective. The student's offer to bring a sari from Delhi gave her relief from the feeling of guilt and failure. I emphasized that any of us, including I, might have done the same. The emotional pressures in such a situation are intense. I was concerned to counteract the potential for shame in the students who felt they did not know what to do, or had done the wrong thing.

I also emphasized that, especially at first, the villagers who had understood that the students were there to help might not have a very precise idea as to how they would help or what kind of help they might provide. Often, the first impulse is to seek immediate resolution to the most pressing problem, whatever that might be. The idea of "help" may at first understandably evoke a variety of longings for

direct sustenance. Acceptance of the kind of help that the students and NGO workers can provide requires an acceptance that the most immediately and obviously
needed kind of help will not be provided.

I then asked the students how, in the light of these points, they thought one
might respond to such a woman asking for money to rebuild the shed. There was
silence in the room. After some time, I made a suggestion:[1] What if one said "you
know, I would really like to help you out in this way, but it is not my function here
to help with money. Rather, once you have found a way to rebuild the shed, I can
do thus and so." I said that what guided this potential intervention was my wish to
acknowledge both that I would like to help with money (I accept and resonate with
the need you are calling to my attention), but I have a limited and very specific
way I can help. This statement might help the students live with the anxiety that
they might be perceived as withholding.

There were a number of ways in which I felt that my psychoanalytic orientation
helped me to help the students in this session. Most prominently, I felt that my experience doing psychoanalytic therapy had trained me to tolerate and work with the feeling that I was not being helpful, or helpful enough. I had been through that guilt and
anxiety many times with help from my teachers and supervisors and the field itself;
I tried to convey some of that understanding to the students. I also felt that I had
been trained to recognize psychic multiplicity and complexity. I knew that one's wish
to help with money was not undone by declining to provide money. The paralyzing
anxiety in such a situation often derives from the fear that one will be perceived as,
indeed that one is, in fact, willfully depriving. I also felt that my psychoanalytic background made me aware of the potential for shame among the students who felt they
"did not know what to do," as they would also have to be sensitive to the potential for
shame among the villagers who had so many needs that would not be met.

Another issue that came up around this village-level work had to do with
the opposition of family members, especially husbands, to women's economic
empowerment and work outside the home. One case in particular was mentioned
in which an alcoholic husband regularly beat his wife when she went out to the
self-help group meetings. As a result, she stayed away from meetings. I asked if
the group leader were a man or a woman, and if it would be possible to assign a
male/female team to address the family problem. It appeared that, generally, group
leaders do not intervene in family conflicts around the women's activities, but
encourage the group members to address the problem within the village. I said I
thought that having a male worker talk to the husband might be helpful, since a
man could say, "look, I know how it is. You are used to your wife being home,
cooking your meals, taking care of the children. But if she succeeds with this side
business, it will help in the following ways." At this point, the student involved
said that the husband in question actually accused his wife of having an affair
with the male group leader. I said that we now had a concrete illustration of the
potential advantage of males and females working together with the women. On a
symbolic level, the male leader would be seen as a part of a couple with the female
leader. He would appear as less of a threat to the husband.

The group of students then reminded me of the husband's alcoholism. I said this was a significant problem, that alcohol rehabilitation was, in itself, a complex field. Here we had run into another problem that this project most likely could not address or solve. One student said that other villages in the project had succeeded in closing down the stores that sold beer in the village. Another student said that even if this could be accomplished, there was no way to keep alcohol out of the hands of an addicted alcoholic. The price of alcohol would probably just increase, making the problem even worse. At this point, my comfort with feeling helpless in the face of intractable problems was tested. I did feel a sense of solidarity with the students who were doing what they could, and who had succeeded in impressing me with the magnitude of the challenges they faced.

## Note

1   I now see, as I write, that there was a parallel process; whereas I wanted to promote self-sufficiency in the class, I also felt tempted to provide them with an answer! I could not formulate this thought at the time, even in my own mind.

# Chapter 4

# Culture and Community-Based Work

There has been relatively more concern with culture among those who do community-based work. The idea that economically and politically disadvantaged communities are more culturally diverse, while incidentally valuable in stimulating interest in culture among those who work there, is based on a false and damaging premise. The premise is that people who are non-white are per se diverse. This idea arises from the cultural presumption (in the United States) that whiteness is not itself a multidimensional cultural and ethnic location. Whiteness, however it is defined, arrogates to itself the sense of being the "standard" or unremarkable baseline from which people "of color" (itself a false notion, since no one is literally white until they die, so everyone has color, and even white is a color) deviate. People who are not included in the category of "white" show up as ethnic or having a culture, while those who are classified as white show up as simply the norm. This way of thinking has a damaging effect, in that a norm automatically creates deviation, and deviation easily slides into deviance. When there is the normal norm, and the deviant "other," the stage is set for denigration, dehumanization, and exploitation. The presumption of a norm and deviation from the norm shows up in the literature on culture in two major ways. The first is the discussion of various nonmainstream ethnic and cultural groups, and only nonmainstream ethnic and cultural groups, in terms of their cultural characteristics, without identifying the cultural vantage point from which the author is observing and characterizing. Clinicians, normally of middle class socioeconomic status, working in public clinics, commonly bemoan missed appointments or the lateness to appointments of their patients, who are likely to be of lower socioeconomic status and/or people "of color." In the context of frustration and conflict, or bemusement, around timeliness, denigrating generalizations might be made about the sense of time in this or that ethnic or socioeconomic group. Rarely is it acknowledged that the middle class sense of time in the United States or Northern Europe, to which most therapists subscribe, can be seen as obsessively exact, sometimes at the expense of the human needs of the people concerned. The clinic itself is likely to be organized around the principle that time is money. The clinicians, if they did not already keep close track of time by virtue of culturally syntonic personality characteristics, are required to do so by administrative pressures to have high numbers of

*agreed*

billable visits. In this context, patients may be seen by clinicians as dysfunction-
ally oblivious to time, while patients may see clinicians as overly focused on time
at the expense of responsiveness to their needs. Time, of course, has many levels
of meaning. Promptness can convey, and be read as, respectful and caring, or as
rigid and insensitive. Flexibility in time can be read, likewise, as responsive to the
needs of the other, or as careless and inattentive. When there is polarization around
these issues, people may retreat to culturally stereotypic generalizations about the
other that posits a norm or a desirable way of considering time in relation to other
factors, and dismisses the other as deviant. If, however, one considers that there
is no "normal" way of dealing with time, only differences and similarities, the
question in each case is how will two or more people come to an approach to time
that works for both of them? How will they find common ground, or a negotiation
of differences? What sense of time works in a particular circumstance? What are
the pragmatic considerations? This approach takes the normalizing, judging, and
assessing function out of the picture in favor of a pragmatic approach. Judgment
instead of judging.

The approach advocated here requires that anyone who writes about culture
first locate her own cultural position as best as she can. The problem here is that
each of us is probably one of the worst people to say anything about his own
cultural location. This is because most of us take for granted as "normal" that
with which we grew up, that which is normative for our own culture. The more
homogenous the cultural surroundings, the more one tends to take one's own way
of seeing the world for granted. Thus, we all need feedback from others to get a
perspective on our own individual and cultural ways of being. The understanding
of culture, crucially including our own cultural location, only emerges from dialogue. This is true in life, and it is true in clinical work. Those who expose themselves reflectively to a variety of cultural differences are best positioned to have a
perspective on cultural similarities and differences. Here is a potential synchrony
of community-based work and psychoanalysis, valuable to each. Community-
based clinicians engage people from a variety of cultural backgrounds, while psychoanalysis provides the tools for exploring clinical interactions for what happens
when worlds of meaning engage each other.

People who work clinically in the community engage their clients or patients
in a wider variety of settings than do clinicians who restrict their work to their
offices. Community-based clinicians might see their patients in patients' homes or
elsewhere in their neighborhoods. Privacy and confidentiality are less protected.
Sessions may take place in a patient's living room, or bedroom, or the broom
closet of a school, or a corner of a classroom, or a corner of a day room on a hospital ward. There may be intrusions of a mother or a child or another patient, and
other various kinds of interruptions. The clinician, who may even live in the same
community as the patient, is challenged to find a way to occupy a professional
role in the midst of the hurly burly and confusion of a patient's home or school or
a hospital ward. There may be confusion as to what the function of the clinician
actually is, in the minds of both patient and the clinician herself. Is the clinician a

psychiatrist who dispenses medication, a social worker who can help with housing or insurance, or cash? Is the clinician an agent of the state or city, someone who could take her children away, judge her adequacy as a parent or a person, help her get services, or take resources away from her? Does the patient/client want the intervention of the clinician, or is the presence of the clinician unwelcome, or is the matter still unsettled? Is the intervention voluntary or involuntary? How does the clinician see herself in the eyes of the client/patient? Does she feel welcome or unwelcome? How does she feel about being welcomed or regarded as a dangerous intruder, or about having to establish that she is there for a benevolent purpose, perhaps when she is not sure in her own mind whether her intervention is in the best interest of the client/patient?

The list of possible scenarios in community-based work could be multiplied endlessly. My main point is that, given the complexities of clinical and nonclinical work in the community, the psychoanalyst's skills at keeping track of the emotional interaction are all the more necessary for keeping one's head above water.

# Chapter 5

# Psychoanalysis, Community-Based Clinical Work, and Culture

## The Three in Interaction

We have looked at the ways in which psychoanalysis can be useful in community-based work, and we have noted the ways that a wider community involvement can be helpful to psychoanalysis and psychoanalysts. We have considered the limitations in how culture is dealt with in the literature of psychoanalysis and in the literature deriving from community-based work. Now, we will turn to the interaction among these three factors. How does cultural context modify the way psychoanalysis shows up at a given time and place? How does culture modify the form community-based work takes?

Consider some instances, anecdotes, which illustrate how psychoanalysis and community-based work show up in the various worlds of meaning constituted by cultures. We start with Freud and the culture of Vienna in the late nineteenth century. As noted above, Freud (1925) himself commented that his status as a Jew, a cultural outsider, contributed to his ability to notice and comment on the mainstream culture. We can presume that he had a special perspective on the hidden sexual element that was hypocritically denied in Viennese upper class society of the time. Sexuality was attributed to Jews, who then came to embody and speak for the denied sexuality among non-Jewish Viennese (Gilman, 1993). Freud shocked his society with his revelation of the sexuality of children, while exposing the sexual exploitation of children (even if he went on to deny the adult's role and responsibility). Through the lens of the postfeminist West, we can now look at this material and see that Freud was not noticing, and thus colluding with, the exploitation of women as well. For example, Freud (1905, p. 27) saw only Dora's sexual impulses in her account of her father's exploitation of her sexual appeal as her father offered Dora as a lure and compensation to the husband of the woman with whom he was having an affair.

Gilman (1993) notes that the denigration of women contained in Freud's notion of penis envy and other concepts represented his displacement of the denigration of the Jew, transferring the image of weakness and inferiority onto women. Through an Indian cultural lens, Bose challenged the universality of Freud's notion of castration anxiety, pointing out to Freud in a series of letters that castration anxiety did not exist, or did not take the same form, among Indian men since in India, men were less terrified of their "feminine" sides (Indian Psychoanalytic

Society, 1999; Kakar,1997). Kakar (2008), also looking at Freud from an Indian perspective, emphasizes not the boy's conflict with the father so much as his "maternal enthrallment" and its sequelae. Whether one regards these commentaries on Freud's work as valid or not, they highlight the cultural embeddedness of Freud's ideas as well as that of the commentators.

As European culture evolved and changed, psychoanalysis evolved in tandem. World War I had a tremendous influence. The impact of the pervasive death and destruction shows up in Freud's (1919) positing of a death instinct, which formed the basis of Melanie Klein's later reformulation of the essential conflict of the human mind as that between love and destructiveness. The dispersal of the European Jewish analysts, mostly to the United Kingdom and the United States, also resulted in profound cultural influences on the way psychoanalytic theory and practice developed. As noted above, psychoanalysis in the United States became a private medical practice under the influence of capitalism and the market economy. The field also consolidated itself as a privileged one, both in terms of its pretensions to knowledge and its toehold among white, affluent people in the United States.

World War II then had a major impact on the development of psychoanalytic theory and technique. When children were moved away from their parents during the bombing of London, an opportunity presented itself to study the effect of separation from parents on young children. Building on the prior work of Rene Spitz (1965) in Austria on the stages of separation and loss that occurs when babies are deprived of physical contact, John Bowlby (1969, 1973, 1980) detailed the stages children go through under conditions of separation and loss. Anna Freud and Dorothy Burlingham (1943) also studied the reactions of children under these conditions. Up to this point, Freudian analysts had viewed the attachment of children to their parents as primarily driven by libido. Attachment was regarded as a form of libidinal investment. Studies of children separated from parents prompted an understanding that attachment was a need in its own right. This insight paved the way for Object Relations theory to emerge in Britain. A seminal insight was contributed by Fairbairn (1958), who considered that attachment patterns, laid down in infancy and early childhood, accounted for the persistence of dysfunctional, destructive, and painful interpersonal connections. D. W. Winnicott (1956), building on his experience as a pediatrician, maintained that the behavior of the actual mother—not just the internalized mother or fantasies of the mother, as elaborated by his teacher Melanie Klein—had a strongly formative effect on the development of children. Winnicott (1956, pp. 300–305) emphasized the significance of "primary maternal preoccupation" for the healthy development of children. In a word, supplementing or displacing the primacy Freud attributed to drive, or libidinal, development, World War II stimulated thought about the impact of actual relationships with caregivers on children. Along with American interpersonal psychoanalysis, to which we will now turn, these developments set the stage for the evolution of relational psychoanalysis in the United States.

The culture of the Euro-American United States is marked by pragmatism and valuation of objectivity. Along with pragmatism goes impatience and suspiciousness toward abstraction and theory when it does not have clear and immediate practical implications. The metapsychologies of Freud and Klein were not practical enough for the United States psychiatrist Harry Stack Sullivan (1953), who translated many of the Freudian concepts into language that was more experience-near and observable. Anxiety went from being a result of drive-defense conflicts in the Freudian and ego psychological theories, to a feeling transmitted from parent to child. What makes a mother anxious will also make her child anxious. Interpersonal psychoanalysis as it evolved in the United States put the clinical psychoanalytic emphasis squarely on the actual interaction between analyst and analysand, as opposed to the unobservable internal world of the patient. Interpersonal technique, correspondingly, moved from a focus on unconscious fantasy to the ways people selectively inattend to events in the interpersonal world.

This has been a sample of the ways that cultural context influenced the development of psychoanalytic theory and practice. Let us now look at the interactions of culture and community-based work.

## Forms of Healing: Spirit Possession, Summoning of Spirits, Exorcism

In this section, we will consider forms of healing that, at first, seemed exotic and strange to me. As time went on, however, I began to find the familiar in the exotic and strange, and the strange and exotic in the familiar. I start with the way people come to a mosque in New Delhi in states of possession; I then expand the lens to include other forms of "folk" or "traditional" healing practices, including modern, Western scientific forms of medical practice and psychotherapy to which the traditional forms are usually counterposed. I aim to see these latter, to the extent possible, with the eye of one to whom they are strange.

## A Visit to the Nizamuddin Mosque in New Delhi

The Muslim Sabbath begins Thursday evening at sunset. One Thursday evening, I set out for the Nizamuddin mosque in New Delhi with the students and some faculty of the M.Phil. program in Psychotherapy and Clinical Thinking in the School of Human Studies at Ambedkar University of Delhi. As a group, we moved through the narrow streets leading up to the mosque past shops selling spices, jewelry, and fabrics, carried along by throngs of people on their way to the evening prayers that inaugurate the Sabbath. We had come because we knew that "mentally ill" people, or, alternatively, people who were "possessed" by spirits, came to the mosque on Thursday evenings. One of the faculty members was acquainted with a woman whose daughter was among those who attended the mosque in a state of spiritual possession. My colleague explained that the people in a state of possession were generally brought by family members who were feeling helpless and frustrated by the behavior of their loved one.

Upon arriving at the mosque, we entered a room to the side where there were people in various states of possession. All were sitting on the ground behind low tables. One man sat motionless with his head down, remaining that way the entire twenty minutes or so we were in the room. Another sat next to a chain-linked fence, his fingers clinging to the fence in a desperate pose, as if he were imprisoned. Soon, the woman who was known to my colleague entered along with her daughter. We all were introduced, then headed out into the main hall of the mosque where prayers were taking place. As prayers were ending, we arrived at a corner of the hall where people who were possessed were gathered. A man was led up to us; he soon began running from side to side of a narrow space, bouncing off the walls and screaming. As his screams rang out, other people in the vicinity started screaming in resonance. I was reminded of a visit I had made to a mental hospital years ago before the advent of major tranquilizers in the United States.

Soon, the man began taking running somersaults, landing with a boom on the wet stone floor, sliding along, and then jumping up to take one, then another, running jump and somersault. Run, jump, tumble, boom, slide, run, jump, tumble, boom, slide. The man did not seem in any way out of control to me. Although I marveled at the fact that he did not injure himself when he landed so hard on the floor, it was clear that he was in precise control of his body movements. His eyes were quite focused. There was not a wild look in his eyes or his expression. I moved out of his way, but no one seemed alarmed or concerned that he would become violent or in any way dangerous to those who were standing within a few feet of him. Finally, after ten or fifteen minutes of this, another man put his body in the way, and the somersaulting stopped. Meanwhile, the crowd of people who had been praying sat on the floor of the great hall, listening to qawalis (religious songs sung in a Persian-derived traditional style). Across the way, other people in a state of possession could be seen twirling around in a dance to the qawalis. A long line of people snaked around the edge of the room entering and leaving a shrine in the middle of the hall.

It was explained to us that the man somersaulting was possessed by a snake and/ or a woman. When he was told that it was time to stop the somersaults, he said, in a woman's voice, that he needed to do three more in order to bring out the spirit of the snake. He was allowed to do three more, and then he stopped.

In class the next day, it was explained to me that what we had observed was called "peshi," which means, in a generic way, to "present oneself." The word is applied to presenting oneself in a court of law, or in the court of a king. In this context, the spirit was called on to present itself during the Sabbath prayers at the Nizamuddin mosque. There was no healer present, seemingly no idea of exorcism, or cure. The idea was simply for the spirit to present itself, or herself, or himself. I was reminded of conceptions of the psychoanalytic situation as designed to call forth dissociated self-states (Bromberg, 2001). As in the mosque, the analyst neither encourages nor discourages this emergence, but simply creates conditions favorable to its appearance.

## Spirit Possession in India and Around the World

There are many such temples in India and elsewhere around the world where people who are believed to be possessed are brought. Skultans (1987) describes one, the Mahanubhava Temple in Maharashtra state in India. Skultans emphasizes a gendered element in the proceedings at this temple. Most of the possessed people at this location are women who are thought to have taken on themselves a malevolent spirit placed in the family by means of witchcraft in the context of a dispute or vendetta with another family member. Indeed, the women who enter a trance at this temple see it as their duty to channel evil spirits away from their family members. In contrast, the priests at this temple see the women in trance as pathological, as opposed to admirably devoted.

A well-known Hindu temple, of which the deity is the monkey god, Hanuman, is the Balaji temple in Rajasthan. The temple's website (http://www.jaybalaji. com/mehndipur.php) states:

> Balaji temple at Mehandipur in Rajasthan is very Powerful [sic] place. It is believed that the deity in this temple has divine power to cure a person possessed with evil spirit [sic]. Hundreds of 'Sankatwalas', as the possessed people are referred to in local lingo, throng to the temple everyday to offer prayers and have "darshan" [author's note: "darshan" means viewing of the deity]. The temple has also become a home and the last respite for the victims. The "Mahant" of the temple, Shri Kishor Puri Ji, prescribes the treatment. It can include reading holy texts, following a strict vegetarian and simple diet, and even afflicts [sic] physical pain to one's body.
>
> One can witness people going through various physical therapies like keeping heavy stones on their body, on arms, legs and chest, to ease their pain. There are others who inhale the smoke that fumes out of the sweet Patasa's kept on smoldering cowpats. The ones with serious case [sic] of spirit possession, who tend to get violent, are even shackled in chains within the temple premises.

"Dargahs" are Sufi Muslim shrines built at the site of a saint's grave. The saint ("pir") is thought to have healing powers. For example, Saheb (1998) reports on the healing rituals that take place at the shrine of Sahul Hameed Nagore Andovar, a sixteenth-century Indian Sufi saint, in Tamil Nadu, India. The saint is thought to have the power to exorcise "jinns" or "bhuts" (i.e., evil spirits). Poor people from far and wide come to this dargah to pray to the saint, hoping to benefit from his healing power without regard to social class, caste, or economic position since one can stay indefinitely at this and other shrines for free.

Pfleiderer (2006), an anthropologist, studied the manifestation of spirit possession at the Mira Datar Dargah in Rajasthan. Women showed evidence of being possessed through wild bodily movements, screaming, and other vocalizations. Most frequently, the women and their families attributed malevolent spirit possession to "black magic" invoked in the context of feuds by envious or otherwise hate-filled people. Pfleiderer's interpretation, however, was that these women were actually shrewdly dealing with an oppressive circumstance in their lives. Most girls in their mid-teens were expected to get married to a boy or man selected by their families, following which they were to leave home to take up residence in the husband's home dominated by his mother. Being possessed by a malevolent spirit made them undesirable as marriage partners, thus exempting them from the helpless position of a child bride being forced to leave home and live with a man she did not know. Pfleiderer, in a formulation that would sound familiar to a psychoanalyst, believed that these women were enacting a dissociated resistance to losing control of their lives in this way. By contrast, though men were present at the dargah, they rarely showed evidence of being possessed.

Werbner (1998) describes the healing activities at a dargah in Punjab. With a psychoanalytic ear, one can listen to the following account with attention to the nature of the transference relationship to the saint. At the dargah, there is:

> a constant daily flow of supplicants seeking healing for their ailments or divine blessings in their jobs, careers and marital fortunes. The healing powers of the saint are grounded in a belief in his ability to see below the surface, to the occult and social causes of illnesses, the thoughts, feelings and accidental transgressions which have brought about pain, chronic illness, infertility, depression, business failures and so forth. As an agent of God, the saint is able to act on these hidden forces and change the course of natural illnesses and social fortunes.
>
> The saint is visited by both male and female supplicants. They sit at some distance from him. Both men and women expose their faces, the women drawing their veils above their heads. The exposure underlines the belief that the saint transcends sexuality. His persona combines male and female qualities— the gentleness, love and tenderness of a woman with the power, authority and honour of a man [see also Kurin, 1984]. He communicates very briefly with the supplicants, addressing them in short, distant tones. Once they have explained their problem to him, he usually instructs them to perform their daily prayers, sometimes throwing a rolled-up, inscribed paper amulet in their general direction. At other times, he instructs them to collect amulets "outside." Once he has heard a whole round of supplicants (he takes in about ten at a time) he raises his hands in prayer—. Even in these brief interchanges, however, the symbolic transference appears to be very powerful. One can only speculate that for the supplicants his immense healing power derives precisely from his gendered ambiguity: he combines maternal and paternal qualities: he is a maternal father or a paternal mother, protective yet authoritative.

(p. 111)

It seems that, like a psychoanalyst, this saint is thought to be able to see below the surface of the disturbance to hidden thoughts, feelings, and troubling events.

Werbner (1998) describes the exorcism at another dargah. The dead saint whose tomb is located at this dargah is named Bava Gor. The understanding of spirit possession at this shrine is based on a dichotomy between "cool" and "hot" influences, corresponding roughly to a distinction between restraint and passion. She writes

> Bava Gor, the cool saint, is also the saint with the power to overcome and exorcise hot demons. [People] . . . suffering from symptoms of spirit possession . . . are called hajrivale, that is, people experiencing a trance. Hajri literally means "presence" and refers here to the presence of a possessing spirit that manifests itself and speaks when the patient is entranced. . . . At the shrine of Bava Gor, hajrivale are completely left to themselves until the behaviour of the patients indicates that the bhut[1] is ready to leave their body. . . .
>
> The place is considered more important than the individual healer since the sacred area represented by the tombs is imbued with those saintly powers (karamat) that ultimately provide the most effective means of exorcising spirits . . . the shrine appears as a healing space.
>
> At the same time, the shrine is a battlefield where the saints fight directly with the spirits. Proximity to a tomb provokes the spirit to reveal itself, which it often does by shows of resistance. Some hajrivali scream their protest as their relatives drag them close to the tomb, and refuse to drink the water of Bava Gor or eat the ash from his fire—both of which carry powerful healing substances. Some of them spit at the tomb, heap insults upon the saints or boast that they will never succumb. If the initial resistance is broken, patients often remain in a trance induced by hyperventilation for hours. The saint may chase the spirit by making the patient move between the different tombs of the three saints. While the bhut speaks through the mouth of the patient, relatives try to find out its identity and demands. . . . In successful cases, a bhut finally accepts the superior power of the saints and agrees to leave the body of his victim.
>
> (p. 131)

In this example, one sees how the first step in exorcism is to get the demon, the "bhut," to reveal itself so that the influence of the saint can be brought to bear against it. As at the Nizamuddin mosque, I am reminded of the attention devoted to getting the transferential object relations to reveal themselves in psychoanalysis.

Finally, Malik (1998) points out that the healing power of ritual depends on the creation of a liminal temporal space:

> Of particular importance are the ritual periods when secular time is displaced by sacred time and when shrine visitors may be said to be transported into a 'liminal' state of oblivion during the annual feasts. The shrine is an institution which is simultaneously therapeutic, social, economic and political; and in contrast to mosques, it also provides an alternative source of communication and identity.
>
> (p. 188)

Like the psychoanalytic situation, the dargah exists outside the time/space framework of ordinary life, offering the opportunity for change in a setting outside entrenched patterns of behavior, thought, and feeling.

## Spiritual and Psychological Models

With respect to the woman known to my colleague and her daughter at the New Delhi mosque, my colleague explained that the daughter had been married to a man who beat her and was otherwise abusive. This husband had died, following which the daughter's state of possession had gradually ended. My colleague said that when she had tried to make a link between the emotional situation of the abusive marriage and the state of possession, the woman had denied that one had to do with the other. One was an emotional problem, and the other was a spiritual problem. I thought that the explanation of the state of possession in terms of emotions might seem reductionistic to the woman. It might threaten to rob the spiritual form of expression of its power. There was indeed an uncanny power to the enactment I had observed; I could understand the wish and need to maintain this channel of expression and communication alongside a more cognitive and verbal form of expression and understanding. A mental health worker with both a psychological and cultural way of understanding the distress of this woman might attempt to talk with her concerning her feelings about her marriage, the abuse, and the death of her husband, without making an explicit link to the state of possession she presented. In situations where exorcism is the goal, the procedures for exorcising a spirit need not be challenged; the culturally specific way of understanding the disturbed state of the person need not be reduced to the emotional or psychological way of understanding held by the worker, as might be suggested by a linear developmental/diagnostic model in which verbalization or "psychological mindedness" is a developmental achievement. Freud and his early followers tried to translate hysterical or somatic states of distress into psychological states that could then be verbalized, leading to insight. Many authors today (e.g., Krystal, 1988) similarly would see the somatic or dramatic presentation of distress as primitive compared to a verbal, psychological presentation. Correspondingly, some forms of psychotherapy, notably insight-oriented psychoanalytic forms, would see patients who somatize as unsuitable for psychotherapy. By contrast, I suggest that the linear developmental model behind such a judgment is essentially culturally biased. Trying to reduce the cause of a state of possession to a psychological or emotional problem could itself provoke what would then be called "resistance," as the person insisted on the uniquely powerful, more dramatic, modes of expression. The psychoanalytic method has its own way of summoning ghosts, if not spirits (Loewald, 1979), through transference evocation. When the ghosts of dead ancestors can be brought to life in the transference, analysts since Freud have argued that one has the preconditions for a successful analysis. Of course, there could easily be those who would regard this claim as outlandish, indeed primitive, from their own biased and judgmental perspective. One could even regard the snake and the woman who possessed the man at the mosque as representing a split-off feminine or sexual part. One could, within a psychological model, explore the anxiety or conflict behind the disavowal and splitting off of some psychic element without imposing this way of understanding. One must only be willing to respect and give space to a variety of ways of understanding and experiencing the person's distress.

In practice, in many cultural contexts, a place is found for the language of spirit possession *and* verbal language or scientific language. When I worked in a mental health clinic in the Bronx, there were people who would consult our psychiatric clinic only after a local, traditional healer had failed to relieve the symptoms. Or, people would try us first and then, if not satisfied, move on to the local healer. In the spiritual system and form of healing in the Caribbean called *Santaria* or *Espiritismo*, Christian imagery of saints and African gods both appear. People in states of distress who are thought to be in the grip of spirit possession are brought to *espiritistas* in storefront *Botanica*s where a variety of means are brought to bear to diagnose the nature of the offending spirit and to exorcise it. In the Bronx, the psychologists, social workers, and other mental health clinicians would sometimes invite into the clinic an espiritista with whom the person or family had worked. Espiritistas on occasion were known to distinguish between spiritual and psychological problems and refer patients to our clinic. Our lingering bias was evidenced by the fact that, to my knowledge, we never referred our patients to espiritistas, even when we were getting nowhere with our psychologically based modes of treatment.

In many traditional societies, doctors who practice indigenous medicine, doctors who practice Western science-based medicine, and shamans who practice some form of exchange with spirits coexist. In India, there are doctors who practice a traditional form of holistic healing, Ayurveda. There are also doctors who practice Western medicine, as well as shamans who deal with spirits. In the West as well, scientific medicine coexists with Ayurveda, herbal healing, and acupuncture based on traditional Chinese medicine, along with various forms of exorcism. While exorcisms are most common among fundamentalist Christian groups in the United States, upper middle class urban people may well consult an acupuncturist and a holistic doctor (who may or may not be trained in scientific medicine), as well as an M.D. who is trained in Western scientific medicine. In Taiwan and elsewhere in China, according to Ahern (1978), there are Western doctors, Chinese doctors, and shamans. In a study of rural people in Taiwan, Ahern found that people believe there are symptoms with an internal origin, corresponding to Western notions of disease. Then there are symptoms considered to have an external origin (i.e., to have originated in contact with a ghost or other spirit). The default assumption is that symptoms have an internal origin, requiring Western or Chinese medical intervention. If that intervention does not work, people will then consider an external origin, leading them to consult a shaman. Rural people believe there is a world of spirits populated with the ghosts of ancestors, called "yin." The world of the living is called "yang." The two worlds are parallel. Every person and object in the yang world has a match in the yin world. Shamans, or *dang-gi* (Tseng, 1978), will contact gods in a state of trance. The gods reveal to the shaman what evil spirit or ghost has "bumped into" the patient, causing his symptoms. If the gods determine that the symptoms have been caused by evil spirits, then exorcising techniques are employed. Or, if it is determined that the symptoms are caused by ghosts of ancestors who are transmitting a message about some unfulfilled duty, performing the required task (e.g., tending to his grave) will bring about a cure.

Spiro (1978), when discussing the interface of medical and spiritual models in Burma, noted that what would be called "mental illness" in the West is exclusively attributed to supernatural causes in Burma, whereas physical illnesses may have either a natural or supernatural causation. He notes four types of dissociative experiences that are associated with spirit possession, not all of which are signs of mental illness. These are séances, divination (inviting a spirit to visit), shamanistic dancing at ceremonies, and mental illness, when a spirit is thought to *force* itself upon the person. The distinction is that forms of dissociation not associated with mental illness are voluntary. Since mental illness is caused by an external intrusion, Spiro notes: "Whereas in modern psychiatry therapy consists of changing certain pathological processes within the individual, in Burmese medicine it consists of changing certain pathological forces which are external to him" (p. 228). Nonetheless, Spiro finds certain features in common between exorcism procedures and psychotherapy: 1. group support, the "active participation of the patient in speaking the thoughts of the supernatural" (p. 229); 2. the confrontation with the unconscious mind, "for although it is believed that while in trance his words are those of the supernatural, we can safely assume that they are rather the words of his own unconscious" (pp. 229–230); and 3. the personality and role of the exorcist.

## From Spirit Possession to Psychoanalysis: From Community-Based Healing to Office-Based Healing

The notion that people can be possessed by spirits of various sorts is not unique to India, and it is not restricted to "premodern" societies, or "premodern" elements in a society. Levack (2006) has documented belief in spirit possession in Europe and North America from Biblical times to the present. His study tracks the evolution of notions of spirit possession in Christian and Jewish religious contexts through the Enlightenment with its rejection of the religious perspective in favor of a scientific one. Reading Levack's account of spirit possession in medieval Europe, with Asian (Indian and Chinese) notions of spirit possession in mind, one is struck by how much more skepticism exists in Europe compared to Asia about the existence of spirits and their power to possess humans. Skepticism is a function of the Enlightenment-born split between rationality and irrationality. This split creates a need to distinguish between that which is rational and that which is irrational. The scientific method, with its empirical evidence-based approach, then recommends itself as a way to sort out the rational from the irrational, the true from the false, and belief which is based on reason from that which is based on faith or emotion. In Europe, the very behaviors that, in a religious context, were explained as evidence of spirit possession were then explained, in a scientific and medical context, as evidence of illness. Note how in the post-Enlightenment account, the "pathological" replaces some combination of "false" and "evil." The language of good and evil, of sin and virtue, of God and Satan, gave way to the various languages of the science of the time, including notions ranging from neurological injury or weakness, to Freud's ideas of the interplay between energic forces. In Freud's hands, the language of spirit possession gave way to the language of repression, of dissociation, and of energically charged impulses clashing with the counter-forces of repression. The metaphor of the demon and demonic possession is ultimately replaced by the metaphor of the split-off self-state. In the following quote from Bromberg (2001, p. 125), imagine the split-off mental state as parallel to the demon in the religious or spiritual world-view

> —a view of the mind as a continuation of discontinuous, shifting states of consciousness with varying degrees of access to perception and cognition. Some of these self-states are hypnoidally unlinked from perception at any given moment of normal mental functioning—while other self states are virtually foreclosed from such access because of their original lack of linguistic symbolization.

Quoting Breuer, Bromberg (2001, p. 127) emphasizes that Breuer explained, "the importance of autohypnosis in the genesis of hysterical phenomena . . .'rests on the fact that it makes conversion easier and protects (by amnesia) the converted ideas from wearing away—a protection that leads ultimately to an increase in psychical splitting.'"

Hysteria is the bridge concept between the religious/spiritual[2] and scientific worldviews. On one hand, hysterical symptoms appear similar to the strange behavior typical of states of possession such as seizures, outbursts of violent behavior, and various forms of fugue states, speaking in "tongues" and so on. Alternatively, such behaviors were also typical of medically pathological conditions associated with lesions in the nervous system. Charcot, a neurologist and Freud's teacher, understood such behavior for which no physical cause could be found as reflecting an underlying hereditary nervous weakness. Charcot and his colleagues in Paris soon discovered that hypnotic suggestion could produce behavior that appeared to mimic hysterical symptoms (Makari, 2008). Hysterical symptoms were found to emerge from the dissociated state produced by hypnotism. Mesmer (1814) had developed a theory of "animal magnetism," the forerunner of hypnosis, following which results could be obtained similar to those obtained by exorcists in cases defined as caused by spirit possession. Mesmer's theory and technique were rejected in Vienna as too spiritual, but his work caught on in France. There, Charcot went further to consider that dissociated states could be produced by various forms of trauma. Finally, Charcot and his colleagues tried to cure people in the grip of hysterical illness by talking, by "therapeutic suggestion" (Makari, 2008, p. 20), to counter what was assumed to be auto-suggestion in states of dissociation. With this "talking cure," the stage was for Freud to develop his particular version of the etiology and talking cure of hysteria. Aron (1996) documents how Freud's turn from hypnosis to free association also reflects his democratic and anti-authoritarian preference for listening and learning, his spirit of scientific inquiry, his interpreting unilaterally to the patient, as well as his effort to exercise therapeutic power. Underlying all these developments, Makari (2008) suggests there was an anticlerical political agenda: "the miraculous and demonic would be exposed as simply hysterical" (p. 17). Several strands of cultural change in Europe come together here: the move away from faith-based sources of knowledge, the anticlerical attitude with the antiauthoritarian, democratic spirit, the reliance on evidence rather than dogma, and the unilateral manipulation of the patient in altered states of consciousness. Benjamin (2001, p. 46) captures the multidimensional complex of transformations taking place as spiritual healing came together with science in the form of psychoanalysis:

> The psychoanalytic doctor is less like a chemist than like the priest who must encounter the demonic in order to exorcise it. Indeed, it turns out that psychoanalysis can refuse hypnotism and faith healing precisely because the same force reappears in the transference; as Freud (1921) will say later, it is only a step from being in love to being hypnotized. *For that matter, how could any German speaker miss the connections between healing (heilen), holy (heilig) and redeemer (Heiland)*.

(emphasis added)

By the same token, however, hypnosis became problematic for those who were trying to establish their scientific credentials precisely because of its link to the trance states associated with spirit possession and exorcism, and not only because of its purportedly unscientific mechanism of action via suggestion. Roth (2001) suggests that Charcot's work appealed to Freud in part because he found a way to make hypnosis acceptable from a scientific point of view. Roth quotes Anne Harrington:

> Charcot manages, in one fell swoop, both to give an aura of medical respectability to a formerly shunned and suspect subject, and simultaneously to stake a clear claim to the medical profession's exclusive competency to deal with this subject.

(Roth, 2001, p. 173)

Ownership of the ability to define trance states was clearly a matter of great significance in a time of contest between science and religion. In a religious context, trance states can be seen as holy; they can give access to the divine, to communication with God or the gods, to spiritual insight. In a traditional context, trance states associated with panic and disruption are likely to be seen as a function of possession by evil spirits, often orchestrated by neglected ancestors or envious members of the family or community, rather than as a function of a disordered psyche. The cure, accordingly, has to do with propitiation of ancestors or exorcism of the offending spirits. In some contexts, the cure of disturbing altered states of consciousness is seen as offering entree into a status as healer. In a medical context, disturbed or anxiety-ridden altered states are likely to be seen as only a sign of individual disorder, as psychopathological. In translating trance into the state of free association, Freud managed to bring altered states of consciousness into a scientific context, while retaining the notion that such states can provide access to a charmed, though desacralized, realm. It should be noted, as well, that trance states are more likely to be valued as part of spiritual development when there is community support and a cultural framework within which they are meaningful. Individuals in trance states on their own, or when culturally derived meaning is absent, are more likely to feel, and to be perceived as, only crazy.

In addition to altered states of consciousness, Freud undertook to encompass sacrifice in his scientific/medical/psychological theory. Kiev (1972) states that, in traditional sacrificial rites around the world, "there is usually a god, a spirit, or a supernatural being, who is either the victim or the recipient or the beneficiary of some offering" (p. 124). The evil spirit possessing a person may be transferred onto an animal that is then killed or expelled as a scapegoat. Kiev also cites cases in which the sacrificed animal symbolizes an enemy who is injured or killed vicariously. Freud (1913) brought animal sacrifice into the domain of psychoanalytic thought with his idea that the sacrificed animal represented the father—the primal leader of the horde who had been murdered by the (male) members of the clan. This act is represented in the killing of the substitute animal, which is then eaten in an act of identification, via incorporation, with the father. Again, Freud takes a phenomenon that had had religious, spiritual, and supernatural meaning in a religious context and transformed it into a desacralized act with a fundamentally psychological meaning displacing the religious one.

One other aspect of cultural change should be noted at this point. Dissociation in contemporary psychoanalytic writing can refer both to the normal multiplicity of self-states described above by Bromberg (1998, 2001) and the traumatically induced splitting of consciousness he also describes as protecting the normal state of consciousness from being overwhelmed by unthinkable events and interactions, like physical and sexual abuse. With the various waves of feminist consciousness rising in the late nineteenth and twentieth centuries, some treatment of women that had been taken for granted or denied in patriarchal society came to be seen as egregious abuse and exploitation. An often-cited example, noted above, concerns the way that Freud (1905) took as unremarkable the treatment of Dora by her father in offering her sexually to Herr K. to cover up his affair with Frau K. From a contemporary point of view around the world, many cases of hysteria or spirit possession can be seen as a response or a protest against oppressive and abusive treatment that was not defined as such in the cultural context of the time. Phenomena that had previously been seen as the product of invasion by alien spirits could now be seen as evidence of a traumatically induced splitting of the personality. Freud's culturally syntonic blind spot in this respect joined with his medical orientation to produce his drive theory, according to which hysterical symptoms came to be seen as the product of a clash between instinctual sexual and aggressive forces within the person and defenses against the awareness of those forces, also within the person. Freud's "economic theory" of clashing forces borrows the language of physics, a scientific language, to explain the very same splits within a person that could be seen as possession by an alien spirit in a religious or spiritual context, or as a function of intolerable oppression that could not be spoken about from a more culturally oriented point of view. Exorcism gave way to hypnosis and then to free association in the effort to call forth the alien or dissociated element to be known, driven away, dispelled, or perhaps communicated with.

As noted, the Enlightenment entailed a rejection of religiously based faith and belief in supernatural beings and spirits in favor of rationality and a focus on the phenomenal world. Once science acquired a status as *the* valid way of knowing and controlling the world, the scientific method became the favored way of checking with nature, as it were, to see if a way of understanding was valid or misguided. Within a framework of "progress" that came with science, evolutionary theory, and the industrial revolution, faith came to be seen as "primitive" (Brickman, 2003) or less evolved. Science, with its method based on skepticism, and technology with its belief that what was true was associated with what worked (or "cured" within a medical framework), came to be regarded as "advanced." Peoples, ways or being, and worldviews were all ordered and ranked along linear lines of development under the regime of progress. Colonialism, racism, sexism, and nationalism were all justified based on the presumed superiority of European and "white" peoples and men over Asian, African, and Latin American peoples and women. Aron and Starr (2012) have documented how psychoanalysis evolved under the influence of Jewish efforts, particularly Freud's effort to disassociate himself from a devalued image of the Jew, especially the Eastern European Jew, as primitive, in fin de siècle Europe. Aron and Starr show how Freud and his followers took pains to base psychoanalytic theory and practice on an Enlightenment-based value system favoring objectivity, at the expense of a value system favoring experience, subjectivity, human interaction and human influence.

In many non-European cultures, the rational-irrational split did not take hold in such a thorough going or dogmatic way. In Europe, the splitting of rationality from irrationality, between that which is true and that which is false, has early roots. In the monotheistic religions, there is only one true God. All other gods are false. Aristotelian logic, further, specifies that A and not-A cannot both be true. One is true and one is false. Combine these exclusionary notions of truth and falsehood with philosophical empiricism, and you have a commitment to the modern scientific method. In India, in Hinduism in particular, there are many valid gods. Islam, though monotheistic, has been, to a degree, absorbed into the Indian pantheon of gods and beliefs. Sufi saints, such as Kabir, are claimed by both Hindus and Muslims for example (Saheb, 1998). It is important not to engage in further splitting at this point by dichotomizing Europe from India with its tolerance for paradox and multiplicity. On the other side, Indians have dichotomized around gender and caste in extreme ways, while Europeans made room for a form of polytheism (the Father, Son, Holy Ghost, and the Virgin Mary) in the way they absorbed monotheistic Judaism.

Be that as it may, any dichotomy between scientific and religious/spiritual values and worldviews is ultimately untenable. Science is based on faith in reason, and religion has often justified itself based on empirical data (e.g., Christ's healing of the sick). Dichotomous thinking in itself is closely associated with the categorization processes endemic to scientific and rational thinking. Obeyesekere (1978) has documented how medical theory and practice based on modern science coexists with traditional holistic belief systems like Indian Ayurveda or the Chinese theory of yin and yang, as well as with supernatural belief systems like spirit possession. Obeyesekere believes that Western, evidence-based science has the last word as to what is effective in treating disease, but that people's beliefs are real to them and must be respected in medical practice. But consider a sentence like the following in Obeyesekere (1978): "All cultures, including popular cultures in the West, have conceptions of the human body which from our contemporary scientific knowledge are false. Though objectively false from our viewpoint, they are subjectively true from the point of view of members of the culture" (p. 257). This statement begs the question as to whether "subjective" reality can have a role in causing and curing disease. Obeyesekere seems to privilege objective reality on an epistemological basis, while granting subjective reality the power to make people ill and to cure them. He continues, "Physical illnesses exist within the organism, even if they are caused by external agents like supernatural beings (or germs)" (Obeyesekere, 1978, p. 257).

Here is where psychoanalysis comes in. Benjamin (2001) points out that psychoanalysis both reinforced and undermined the dichotomy between rationality and irrationality, read as emotional or impulse-based, in lieu of what would have previously been seen as faith-based.[3] Freud reinforced the split by positing healing power to reason, in the form of the analyst's interpretations, against the pathogenic anxiety-generating impulses based in the id. He also reinforced and exploited the status of the scientific method by insisting that the analyst must take a strictly objective (neutral) stance in relation to the patient. The psychoanalytic patient was all subjectivity, while the analyst was all objectivity. At the same time, by emphasizing the ubiquity of the unconscious, Freud undermined man's (in both the generic and gendered senses) pretensions to control of his own mind, his own capacity to be objective in relation to his own mind. Freud never posed, much less answered, the question as to how the analyst could ever be so objective if the unconscious were as ubiquitous as he posited. Or one might ask whether there was an exception to be made for psychoanalysts, or perhaps uniquely for Freud himself.

Benjamin (2001) emphasizes that psychoanalysis, by virtue of this paradoxical relation to subjectivity and objectivity, was in a good position to work within this borderland to reconcile the splits that had been drawn by the Enlightenment. Such efforts at reconciliation, at healing in a number of senses, occur in every analytic treatment as the analyst struggles with his subjectivity in relation to the patient's. This tension also exists and plays itself out as psychoanalysis tries to define and redefine itself in the context of cultural shifts and fashions. Recently, for example, psychoanalysis and many other fields have made major efforts to embrace science, its method, and its basic skepticism as efficiency and functionality has become increasingly valued in societies around the world. Embracing the scientific-medical model, psychoanalysis has developed an intensely ambivalent relationship to anything smacking of emotion, intuition, and direct experience, as well as to spirituality and faith. While some psychoanalysts seek status for their field as "evidence based," others exhibit receptivity to alternative healing methods, yoga, and Eastern spirituality. All along, even as cost-effectiveness reigns supreme in many sectors of the culture, large numbers of people continue to embrace religion, spirituality, experience, and emotion-based ways of knowing the world and finding meaning in their lives. Some rapprochement has occurred between objective/scientific and subjective perspectives as scientific research has documented various mind-body connections, for example, the placebo effect (Harrington, 1997), the Type A personality and heart disease (Steptoe & Molloy, 2007), the effect of emotional states on health (Salovey, Rothman, Detweiler, & Steward, 2000), and so on. Within psychoanalysis, Mitchell (1993) argued that, in recent years, the value system underlying much psychoanalytic work has shifted from one based on functionality and cure, to one based on the search for meaning in life. Psychoanalysis itself has been called into question by a progression in the evolution of the scientific perspective toward empirically validated treatments. Nonetheless, in the supposedly relatively rational Western world, Eastern religion, yoga, meditation, holistic medicine, and fundamentalist Christianity and Judaism all thrive. Meanwhile, in Asia and Africa, forms of fundamentalist religion based in Islam, Hinduism, and other religions flourish alongside of, or in competition with, "Western" notions of material and scientific progress.

As techniques of exorcism evolved and transformed into hypnotic methods and then into talking cures such as psychoanalysis, one can track various other ways in which notions with roots in a religious or spiritual language came to be reformulated in scientific or psychoanalytic language. Aron and Starr (2012, p. 296) call our attention to the Jewish notion of the "dybbuk" (i.e., "a dislocated soul that cannot rest"). The dybbuk seems to be the Jewish concept parallel to the spirits that are spoken of in Christian traditions, as well as in the various forms that appear in Muslim and Hindu contexts. According to Aron and Starr (2012, p. 296 fn.), the motto on Freud's (1900) *Interpretation of Dreams* translates as "stir up the underworld" (i.e., "stirring up the mental underworld in order to get a hearing"). Recall the way the "peshi" process as seen in Delhi's Nizamuddin mosque, noted above (p. 31), was conceived of as promoting the manifestation of spirits in those who were possessed (i.e., for the spirits to get a hearing). Freud compared the "uncanny" feeling that attends the return of the repressed to the feeling of being haunted and tormented by a dybbuk. Loewald (1979) spoke of the psychoanalytic process as one of laying "ghosts" to rest so that, instead of haunting the living as ghosts, they could enrich their lives as ancestors. One might conceive of object relations theory, with its language of internal objects, as a psychoanalytic reformulation of the language of ghosts, spirits, and dybbuks. Goldstein (2001) notes that, in the case of Nanette Roux, Bertrand (1826) had tried to find common ground between medical/scientific language and the language of religion by replacing the world "catalepsy" in earlier descriptions of the case with "ecstasy." Goldstein points out that ecstasy had long been associated in the Christian tradition with such intense spiritual experiences as divine inspiration and mystical union with a transcendent object. "Bertrand wanted to exploit the term's religious connotations to argue for the compatibility of science and religion—In making ecstasy a medical category, he intended to affirm simultaneously, first, the subjective authenticity of ecstatic phenomena, second, any religious meaning that the ecstatic might impute to them, and finally their completely naturalistic underpinnings" (Goldstein, 2001, pp. 154–155). Evidently, at the time, it did not seem impossible to think in scientific and religious terms simultaneously. By the time of the case studies of Breuer and Freud (1893–1895) at the end of the nineteenth century, however, the same symptoms were cast in purely scientific terms, though evolving from physical/neurological to psychological and, finally, to social language. Goldstein ends her article about the case of Nanette with the formulation that her symptoms may have expressed in disguised form a wish for personal autonomy generally denied to women at the time. Returning to psychoanalysis, in the words of Goldstein:

> Freud saw the kind of psychological interpretation that he advanced as antithetical to religious interpretation; in the course of elaborating the psychoanalytic theory, he attacked the religious worldview as if the eighteenth century Enlightenment had never occurred. Bertrand, by contrast, intended his insistence on psychological causation as a corrective to the Enlightenment and as a gesture friendly to religion. He wanted to draw from the healing power of *confiance*[4] a lesson about the health-giving nature of traditional Christianity as well as its compatibility with the posture of scientific rigor.
>
> (2001, p. 158)

It is notable that Goldstein, in this passage, sees Freud as still fighting the war between religion and science as if the Enlightenment had not occurred, or had not prevailed. She implies that, from Freud's point of view, the religious perspective on hysteria was alive and well. Freud may have felt that he needed to bend over backward to deny the religious perspective, as Aron and Starr (2012) argue that he bent over backward to deny the Jewish context of his work.

Finally, Goldstein notes that an evolution occurred within the religious perspective in Europe from the language of spirit possession and exorcism, to the language of sin and confession. The possessing spirit is regarded as an objective entity and external to the person. Sin, by contrast, derives from a personal act, one for which the person bears responsibility. Here is a move consistent with psychoanalysis in that it locates the source of symptoms within the personal space of the individual, but in a religious, rather than scientific, framework. The transformations of the cultural meaning of altered states of consciousness that took place in Europe, especially under the influence of Christianity, is well illustrated by Kiev (1972) citing Sigerist (1948). Orgiastic Dionysian rites involving music and dancing, of Greek origin, were suppressed by Christian authorities. Driven underground, they came to be defined as sinful. Later, in a medical context, such orgiastic behavior came to be defined as disease—the result of poisoning by a tarantula bite. Orgiastic rites survive in Southern Italy in the form of a dance—the tarantella. Kiev (1972), in a similar vein, reports that peyote, previously viewed by Mexican people as a divine substance, was reframed by Christian missionaries as the "the work of evil" (p. 111).

There are other reformulations of concepts with roots in Christianity into psychoanalytic language. These are comprehensively discussed by M. Hoffman (2010) as noted above. Fairbairn's (1958) language, for example, was at times explicitly religious. He wrote of the psychoanalytic process as more akin to "salvation" than to cure, comparing bad internal objects to the devil. He explained people's otherwise inexplicable attachment to a bad, or guilty, sense of self in terms of a "moral defense" in which people would prefer to be a bad or guilty person in a world ruled by God, than to be a good person in a world ruled by the devil.

For all the concerted effort to establish psychoanalysis as a scientific theory and method, to differentiate it from religious or spiritual theories and methods of healing, there are many parallels that can be drawn. These parallels have the character of an idea or method, transplanted into a different cultural and historical context, yet bearing the mark of the earlier concept or method. For example, consider, as noted above, the traditional concept of "ancestor" in relation to the psychoanalytic concept of "internal object." In many traditional theories of healing, the problem is defined as a curse or spirit possession consequent to the displeasure of ancestors. Ancestors may be displeased because of neglect of one's duties toward them (e.g., failure to care for a grave, or some behavior regarded as a sign of disrespect toward an ancestor). As noted above, despite differences in many particulars, "ancestors" are easily translatable into the psychoanalytic notion of "internal objects"—like ancestors or the residues of past relationships. Loewald (1979) made the parallel explicit in comparing the psychoanalytic process of transference to a process in which ghosts, i.e., the unburied dead, are converted to ancestors, spirits from the past that can enrich, rather than haunt, the present. Contemporary psychoanalysts tend to think of internal objects as haunting the present via the lasting attachment patterns that are established in early life, as opposed to the effect of failing to do one's duty toward ancestors; yet, one might say, in a traditional context, duty largely defines attachment. Speaking of transference, there are parallels that can be made between the type of relationship referred to as "transferential," and the kind of relationships that exist between people and healers (shamans, exorcists, priests, gurus, and so on) in various traditional cultural contexts. What appears similar is a mystique or authority attributed to the healer, which, in psychoanalytic language, can be easily thought to derive from a parental model. By way of contrast, specific relational patterns are not thought of as defining the relationship to traditional healers, yet the mystique of the healer elevates what happens with him above and beyond the events of ordinary life with special healing power (Hoffman, 1998), whether in a psychoanalytic or traditional, religious, healing context. Yet another parallel is the notion of "wounded physicians" or wounded healers (Jung, 1954, pp. 115–116) in traditional and psychoanalytic contexts. In many traditional contexts, those who have been possessed by spirits, and undergone an exorcism, are considered chosen for the role of shaman (Kiev, 1972). The process of suffering and healing amounts to the selection process and training for shamans in a variety of cultures, as the training analysis is an important part of the training of psychoanalysts. States of possession, or psychosis, or altered states of consciousness are considered variously signs of disorder, holiness, or the potential gift of healing power across a variety of cultures. Another parallel is the role of dreams as entree to the realm of spirits, ancestors, or the unconscious, as the case may be. Kiev (1972) points out the access to the realm of spirits and ancestors is obtained through dreams among the Luzon people of the Philippines, and the Mohave tribe of Native Americans, among many others. He notes that, in Haiti, the call to become a voodoo priest is most commonly found in dreams. In this latter connection, there is some notion of dual realms, conscious-unconscious, yin-yang, and so on with ordinary life, or life in an ordinary waking state of consciousness, on one hand, and the realm of spirits, ancestors, and internal objects on the other. Finally, Frembgen (1998), speaking of majzubs, in Pakistan, who are thought to be possessed by holy spirits, notes:

> Advocates of Western orthodox biomedicine might suggest as a diagnosis that many majzubs are actually schizophrenics, hysterics, epileptics or autistics. Beyond the questionable transfer of Western medical concepts and terms to another culture, what such a diagnosis misses are the emic perspectives on charismatic "possession." In the Islamic world, a majzub means a person being in a permanent state of ecstasy and divine emotion, in most cases enraptured since birth, but sometimes in response to dramatic visions or far-reaching experiences of the soul. The Arabic term majzub is derived from the verb yazaba—jazaba in the vernacular—meaning "to be attracted to" or "drawn to." A majzub is therefore "drawn" to God. When he follows the divine call, his heart is fully captured and enveloped by the Almighty. Mental disorders prove that his soul is overflowing with God's light and that he is absorbed by him. To draw a comparison with antiquity, epilepsy was called the "holy disease," hence epileptos means in Greek "enraptured" (Benz 1972: 127). In

the language of Christian religious experience, being moved by divine emotions points to the seizing hand of God.

(p. 145)

The dualities that we have noted on various levels are themselves interrogated by Ewing (1998). She attempts to transcend the traditional/spiritual versus modern/scientific dichotomy with close attention to how people actually describe the phenomena under study, with a focus on how the listener, the observer, categorizes the information provided by the informant. In noting the polarized categories used, Ewing hopes to help the reader reflect on, and put herself in a position to transcend, the polarized categories. Consider the following from Ewing (1998):

> It has been noted that in popular Muslim belief madness and feeblemindedness are regarded not as disease, but as a sign that the affected person lives in a state closer to God than do most of us. In my own fieldwork in the vicinity of Lahore, Pakistan, I heard many stories of men and women acknowledged to be mad (pagal) who did such things as wandering the streets half-naked or spouting nonsense. Many people will go up to such unfortunates and touch them to receive God's blessing through them. Among those who could be labelled pagal, there were some—called majzub—who were treated with all the reverence and deference bestowed upon saints. In the Urdu language, the majzub is "one whom God draws to Himself" (Platts 1983:1002). The majzub is one whose speech and actions appear to lack sense because his or her mind has been "burned" by the closeness to God.

(p. 160)

Ewing continues (p. 161):

> But a general statement such as this is, of course, wrong. It highlights (or, rather, creates) a gulf that separates a modern Western discourse that constitutes "mental illness" as an observable, clinical, medical entity (see Foucault 1973) from a Muslim discourse that apparently does not. It obscures the nuances and contextual specificity with which Pakistani Muslims assess and react to those they label pagal. I did not feel a conceptual gulf when I participated in these people's lives and observed their behavior toward those whom they acknowledge to be pagal or majzub, even when I was introduced to the majzub who buzzed at me. Sure, I was startled when the man put his thumb on my forehead, but my nonverbal reaction seemed to be perfectly understandable to my companions.

Is a person mentally ill, or possessed by a spirit, or a holy person? Ewing finds that she, along with her Pakistani informants, is able to tack back and forth between various points of view as long as they don't privilege one perspective as more objectively true than others. The preconception that one point of view is superior to the others in itself creates the dichotomy that is then taken as evidence for a cultural difference, often organized around a hierarchy of objectivity. Ewing links her nonpolarizing point of view to that of Deleuze and Guattari (1983), who critique Western psychiatry for reproducing hegemonic discursive frameworks by rendering the alternative simply primitive or crazy. In a case, Ashiq, cited by Ewing (1998, p. 166 ff.), there were symptoms that lent themselves to a medical understanding (heat stroke), a supernatural understanding (black magic imposed by an envious rival), and a religious one (Ashiq was a saint). Ewing's position is not that the medical explanation is the standard or superior framework for understanding. Nor is it inferior. Rather, the medical and supernatural and religious frameworks coexist fluidly in a way that leaves open the possibility that they could be ultimately subsumed into a larger, inclusive interpretive framework.

## Psychoanalysis and Psychotherapy Exist in Communities: They Isolate Themselves at Their Own Peril

To the extent that psychotherapy, in its various forms, has evolved in accord with a scientific, antireligous, or antispiritual perspective, it has both appealed to and alienated people. It has found a place within some socioeconomic structures (e.g., the free-market economy and the insurance industry), and abdicated its place in others (e.g., the religious and spiritual movements of the day). In the context of the present book, the argument leads to the following point: if psychotherapy and psychoanalysis wish to broaden their appeal in the world at large, to expand beyond the limited present clientele, a reconciliation of the scientific and spiritual worldviews would be a step in the right direction. In other words, I aim to reconsider the parting of the ways that took place when notions of spirit possession were displaced, for some, by medically defined illness. One should notice what and who got lost and what and who were alienated when science and spirituality went in opposite directions. Understanding altered states of consciousness in a religious/spiritual context lives on in all parts of the world. In the twenty-first-century United States, a prominent example is Pentecostalism with its ecstatic rituals involving possession by the divine spirit, healing, and speaking in tongues. If psychoanalysis is to speak the language of the communities in which such religious frameworks live on, the field may have to consider how to reestablish the links between science and religion that were severed in the polarizing movements of the Enlightenment. As I suggest elsewhere in this book, the underlying links can be identified and used as the basis for reconciliation. Psychoanalysis, as a worldview, is especially well suited to this task both because the links between the religious/spiritual and scientific are so evident (e.g., with hysteria as a bridge concept, as noted) and because its dialectical framework (e.g., consciousness-unconsciousness informing and constituting each other) provides an antipolarizing ethos, like that of Ewing (see above).

## Notes

1  "Bhut" means "spirit."
2  While religion and spirituality are related, I use both words to indicate the distinction between religion as a social structure, as in "organized religion," with its regulatory power, and spirituality, as a worldview and way of knowing.
3  When the opposite of rationality is read as faith-based, enlightenment philosophy is deployed against religion; when it is read as emotion or impulse-based, it is deployed to denigrate women and non-European cultures.
4  A term referring to Nanette's confidence in healing techniques of her own devising.

# Chapter 6

# Clinical Work in Communities

Clinical work out of the office in the community is nothing new to the thousands of mental health professionals who work in schools and in hospital inpatient units. For these clinicians, and for others in a variety of settings, there may not be a clear demarcation between in-office and out-of-office work. Many clinicians in institutions have an office available to them. Sometimes the office is shared with one or more other staff, so that at any given moment, a therapist and his patient may be scrambling to find space, sometimes during time that should have been within the session. Sometimes, the patient refuses to come to the office, so that the work ends up taking place in the classroom or in the hospital unit day room, or somewhere in between. Sometimes, there simply is not an office assigned to the clinician at all. One week before I began working at Bronx Lebanon Hospital's Child and Adolescent Psychiatry Outpatient Clinic, I called the Chief of the clinic on some bureaucratic matter. At the end of the conversation, he said, "By the way, you don't have a desk." I said, "Oh, that's okay. I can do without a desk. May I leave my papers somewhere?" He said, "I mean you don't have an office." "Oh, all right . . . I guess." At that point, I had worked for three years as a psychologist in Head Start and was used to catch-as-catch-can space arrangements.

School-based therapists trying to establish some sort of regularity in meetings with their assigned patients have to adjust to the vagaries of classroom schedules, tests, field trips, and teachers who are reluctant for a student to leave class, not to mention a student's reluctance to leave class, with the therapist trying to coax a child out of class in front of teachers and other children, only to find that there is no place to sit except a janitor's closet or a stairwell (Dunn, 2012). School-based therapists also work in the community in the sense that they must take account of the participation of teachers, other professionals like speech and language therapists, occupational therapists, guidance counselors, school administrators, and parents in the lives of the children they see (Jacobs, 2012).

## Psychotherapy in, out of, and around the Office

There are a number of examples of clinicians doing psychoanalytic work out of the office, whether the "office" is the private office or the public clinic office, or a make-shift office in a car, a park, a diner, a fast food restaurant. A recent example of an in-office but community-based project is Mark Smaller's (2012) "Analytic Service to Adolescents Project" in a school in Cicero, Illinois, located just outside of Chicago. The school served high school students who had been expelled from other high schools in Cicero. What is remarkable about this project is the commitment of a psychoanalytic institute, the Chicago Institute for Psychoanalysis, to raise funds from private sources to see forty students in group therapy and eight to nine students in individual therapy, as well as the determination on the part of the organizers to convince naysayers in the Institute that psychoanalytic work could proceed under these conditions.

Ann Marie Sacramone (2012) reported on work done in a preschool located in a neighborhood community center. She was employed in a funded project to provide psychoanalytic consultation to this preschool that served a variety of children, some with special needs, in an inclusive setting. In this center with its enlightened holistic philosophy, Sacramone was enabled to intervene and consult at all levels in the preschool and community center. She consulted preschool teachers and other staff and parents and other family members, while seeing some children individually and in the context of the classroom. Sacramone's perspective was psychoanalytic in the intersubjective, developmental, self-psychological tradition. She considered both the leading edge (developmental potential) and trailing edge (developmental lags requiring remediation) aspects of the child's development. For example, experience with the children with whom she worked convinced her that a child's play can reflect a process of empathic inquiry into the experience of others that can both stimulate development and enrich the environment in which the children are embedded. In this sense, empathic inquiry is an act of social/developmental significance (Ann Marie Sacramone, personal communication, September 23, 2013). In the context of an inclusive setting, she began to consider that interaction between socially open children and socially isolated children could stimulate the social development of *all* children as the more open children engage in an empathic inquiry into the meaning of the behavior of the more withdrawn children. The children engaged in empathic inquiry with each other, sometimes with direct questions, and sometimes by imitating or otherwise joining in the initially socially isolative play of the more withdrawn children. Sacramone facilitated this process of empathic inquiry herself as she participated in the classroom, as well as via the classroom staff with whom she was consulting, and with whom she worked collaboratively in the classroom.

One girl, Pali, was initially seen at age two at the initiative of her grandmother. Pali was socially isolated and prone to tantrums at points of transition. People in her grandparents' generation, living in a third world country colonized by Europeans, were slaves. Opposition to the racist colonial regime led to the murder of Pali's great uncle, while others in the family fled the country. Pali was cared for by a series of childcare workers while her parents worked long hours. The great aunt, Bubba, was concerned about the inconsistency in the care of Pali as caregivers came and went frequently.

Sacramone saw Pali in individual sessions three to four times per week. For one year, Pali did not play with other children. She would create flowers out of manipulative toys, objecting when other children attempted to join her in this constructive play. After a year, she began to connect with other children by sitting in square spaces created by the other children out of blocks. Eventually, this participation led to fantasy play involving Pali and others. Once she broke through her isolation, Pali quickly became a fully engaged member of the classroom community. Her individual sessions moved flexibly and freely between a designated therapy room, the classroom, and other spaces within the community center.

As the time approached when Pali would have to leave the preschool, and her therapist, to begin kindergarten, the therapy became animated with themes of loss and emotional pain. In her play, a terrified doll was made to hang from a precipice. Pali played hide-and-seek games with her therapist. In a beautiful use of the community center space, one day she went to the room where she had attended her first preschool classroom. She entered the classroom, approached and was welcomed into the group of two-year-olds. She announced her summer plans that she was going to Ireland with her grandmother. She took a toy vehicle and stuffed it full of dolls/friends whom she was symbolically taking with her as she left the preschool where she had grown so much. She gave her therapist her own vehicle with two dolls in it. On the day they were to say good-bye, Pali said that they would now go their separate ways, but would meet again. Sacarmone felt that, in this way, the legacy of an intergenerational history of trauma, separation, and loss was being processed and reworked in the developing mind of this little girl.

Consider the use of space in this therapy. Of course, all therapies take place in space; they are affected by the space in which they occur. The private office is the therapist's space; the therapist organizes the experience in many ways that register consciously and unconsciously for both participants. When the therapy takes place out of, or in and out of, the office, space opens up dramatically to include spaces that belong at least as much to the patient as to the therapist. The space may be open space not claimed by either one, explored together. In Pali's case, the space of the preschool was a space/time continuum covering time and space in multiple family/historical and personal dimensions. Such is the richness that can be accessed when we open up our notions about the space in which therapy can occur.

Another therapy in which space played a dramatic role was conducted under the auspices of the "Fostering Connection," a program in New York City to match volunteer therapists with children, adolescents, and families who have been affected by foster care. Willeboordse (personal communication, December 10, 2013) reported on her work with S., a sixteen-year-old boy who was living with his great aunt. S. had been seen in individual therapy by Willeboordse since he was twelve years old. His mother had abandoned him at birth; subsequently, he was placed in foster care. At age three, his grandparents, who were both alcoholic, claimed him. When he was nine years old, his grandmother died of cirrhosis of the liver. Several months following his grandmother's death, S. and his brothers and sister were removed from the grandfather's care as a result of allegations of neglect. S. and his younger sister were then placed to live with his great aunt. S.'s great aunt was also caring for her own five children.

During the first year of therapy, S. came late to Willeboordse's office and talked little. His most common response to questions was to shrug. He and his therapist would play competitive games in the office, sometimes "Spit," a card game during which he would slow down and focus a bit.

Despite his reluctant demeanor, S. continued returning for his weekly sessions regularly. When Willeboordse, somewhat at her wit's end as to how to engage him, would talk about her own experiences in sports, he would perk up, especially when she discussed conflict with her own swimming coach. He lit up noticeably when the topic was boxing.

In the second year of therapy, Willeboordse and S. began to go outside during sessions. In an experimental mode, they once went to the local Barnes and Noble and read together. S. talked more during that one session than he had in any of the four or five previous sessions. Another time, they went to the Rubin Museum of Asian art together. Finally, on another day, they went to a diner for snacks. Subsequent sessions continued to take place in this diner. Outside the office, the focus of the conversations was often S.'s family experiences. In one session in the diner, Willeboordse felt she was learning more about S. and his life than she had during the entire first year in her office. There were two television screens in the diner. In most sessions, much of the time was spent silently watching television until sometimes something on the television news would trigger a conversation, perhaps about police brutality, or a murder, or politics. Unexpectedly, a cooking show brought out a lot of enthusiasm from S. They ordered a spinach feta omelet and ate it together. The next week, S. said he had cooked a spinach feta omelet at home. A rapport developed with the owner of the diner, the waiters, and busboys as they appeared weekly.

Willeboordse met S. weekly in the diner for a year, wondering "Is this what I should be doing?" As a candidate in psychoanalytic training, meeting with her patient in a diner and discussing the news as it appeared on the television felt to her as if she were out on a limb by herself. Something that seemed fundamental about psychoanalysis appeared under challenge as this therapy progressed, even as psychoanalysis seemed the only reliable guide on this uncharted road.

Meanwhile, Willeboordse had occasional conversations with S.'s great aunt, Ms. A. There had been a number of aborted therapies with S. and his family because Ms. A. would stop cooperating with treatment, so Willeboordse knew she had to cultivate her connection with Ms. A. if she was to be able to work with S. However, Ms. A. seemed sullen and irritable with Willeboordse when she tried to reach out to her. Like S., in the early phase of this therapy, she seemed to reject therapy even as she tacitly allowed it to occur.

A particular point of frustration between Willeboordse and Ms. A. occurred when Ms. A. repeatedly took S.'s cell phone away as a punishment for failure to complete household tasks or other infractions. This punishment had no end point, however, as Ms. A. would claim to lose the cell phone, until months later when S. would find a way to lay his hands on a new cell phone, which would promptly be taken away and lost by Ms. A. Willeboordse found this disciplinary regime counterproductive, as S. was unable to stay in touch with Ms. A. when he was out, which led to further infractions. Willeboordse would occasionally try to talk with Ms. A. about this situation, but Ms. A. seemed impermeable to input, insistent on how difficult and recalcitrant S. was, how taking away his cell phone was the only punishment that seemed to affect him. She was willing to consider restoring the cell phone for good behavior, as unlikely as that seemed, if she could only find it. Nonetheless, life and therapy went on in its unconventional way.

In the third year of therapy, S. discovered a magazine written by and for foster youth. He entered a poetry contest, writing a poem about the day that he was removed from his grandfather's home. Although he did not win this contest, efforts to ascertain the results of the contest kept him in touch with the editor, who eventually offered him the opportunity to attend a summer writing workshop with funding. He was the youngest member who attended these workshops. As part of this workshop, he wrote an essay about his life that included a tribute to his therapist. Meanwhile, S. was failing his classes in school.

At one point, Willeboordse decided to take S. to a movie, "Win Win," because the main character's life seemed to have many parallels with S.'s, and she thought seeing the film might stimulate discussion. When the main character became enraged at his mother, S. covered his face. After seeing this movie, S. suggested that they go to another movie together, "Warrior," about a wrestler with family problems, including an alcoholic father, a dead mother, and two brothers who box. Clearly, S. understood that the point of this therapeutic movie watching was to provide a focus for the representation of his own family experience. S.'s identification with the characters in this movie allowed him to talk about emotionally charged events in his life without having to talk explicitly about himself (Willeboordse, personal communication, September 23, 2013).

During this third year, Willeboordse brought S. to a sports program at "Beat the Streets," an athletic program sponsored by a local community center. Amazingly to his therapist, who had contacts at this center, the staff there knew S. Evidently, he had attended this program before, but had disappeared at some point right after winning a state-level prize. Willeboordse, who was an accomplished, world-ranked swimmer herself, reflected sadly on the contrast between the parental support enjoyed by a private swimming student of hers and the way S. had to generate his own motivation and devotion to sports.

In the fourth year of therapy, Willeboordse and S. made a foray into boxing. S. liked boxing and Willeboordse had coached the sport. Once again, as they sparred with each other, Willeboordse wondered at what her analytic superego figures would think of this activity. But, the work seemed to have an analytic logic of its own. S. said, "I want to be really angry when I fight." He and Willeboordse agreed that there's nothing more satisfying than wrestling, especially when you're a really angry person. He quickly declined to box with Willeboordse, however. Perhaps it was too stimulating or physical, or he did not want to reveal his lack of mastery of the sport in front of his therapist, or perhaps he did not want his therapist to be in the superior role of teacher (Willeboordse, personal communication,

September 23, 2013). In any case, this activity was set aside in favor of meetings back at the diner, where the conversations became deeper and richer. In the neutral territory of the diner, S. seems to feel relatively free to explore his feelings in his therapist's presence in response to the wide range of human stimuli on the television or provided by the other diners and staff. For example, he commented at one point that he did not plan to get married because he would not want his wife to leave him. On another occasion, as a blind person entered the diner, S. said that if he were blind, he could not trust people. His therapist responded, "because you check people out with your eyes to see if you can trust them?" to which he agreed.

The kind of out-of-office work conducted by Sacramone and Willeboordse is simultaneously more ordinary and more challenging than office-based therapeutic work. In one sense, anyone can do this kind of work; in another sense, this work is not for beginners. One is called on to behave as oneself, as one might in an ordinary social interaction. At the same time, one is challenged to find a way to utilize such interactions for analytic/therapeutic purposes. One is called on to improvise (as Ringstrom, 2007 argues is the case in the office, as well) in a relatively unstructured environment in such a way as to keep emotional communication (not necessarily verbalized) going. At times, this agenda may entail shadow boxing, going to a movie and discussing it, sitting in a diner and eating, watching television, chatting and bantering with the staff, taking a walk in a community center or school building without knowing for sure where one is headed. Then, whatever happens, one attempts to reflect on it, to make meaning. One makes a comment or responds nonverbally at times, trying to move toward formulation or further development of emotional meaning that may theretofore have been hidden or unformulated, or repressed, or dissociated, depending on how one thinks or the psychotherapeutic language one speaks.

The payoff for this kind of work includes being able to work with people who are otherwise inaccessible to psychotherapy, who may feel unfamiliar with or alienated from the office-based, private practice with which the therapist may feel more comfortable or familiar. Secondly, one expands the range of stimuli for conversation, as when the television or a movie or the community center provides the jumping-off point for emotionally meaningful comments by Pali or S.

## Training in Hospitals

Students in the MA program where I was teaching in India were participating in a one-month rotation in one of two hospitals in Delhi, a government hospital, and a private hospital. They spent a week or so in an outpatient clinic, an inpatient unit, and a day hospital.

One student who was placed in the private hospital finished her inpatient rotation and was about to begin her placement in the day hospital. She explained that the day hospital was in the basement of the building, and that as she descended the stairs, she had a feeling of foreboding, a sense of claustrophobia as she noted that there would be no windows in the basement. When she arrived at the day center, there was a senior intern leading a group of patients, all of whom were considerably older than he was. The student was shocked to see the harsh and disrespectful way that the intern was speaking to his elders, just because they were patients and he had authority over them. He was leading an activity that had to do with the patients writing about how they felt about New Delhi. One patient wrote that there were things that he disliked about New Delhi. The intern scolded him: "What did I tell you? Didn't I tell you to write about things you like about New Delhi?" The intern thought this was outrageously disrespectful to an older person. She said she had been brought up to treat her elders with respect.

I said that I was listening to what she said almost like a dream—that she was descending into the underworld of the unconscious, a la Dante's Inferno, as she approached the Day Program. And what did she find down there? An oppressive defensiveness that made no room for bad feelings and a breakdown of human respect along with the norms with which she had been brought up.

The student knew quite consciously what made her feel badly at the Day Program. What does regarding the imagery she presented as dream-like add to what she already knew in a way that would help any clinical process with which she might become involved there?

Translating the student's account into dream imagery moves the narrative from one having to do specifically with the objective characteristics of this hospital, this Day Program, to a level of broader psychic and social significance. There might be links to personal fears and phobias held by this particular student that might have been triggered by the Day Program. Recognizing her feelings might help her put the anxieties aroused by the Day Program into perspective. Looking at the student's reaction as a subjective one does not make it any less accurate or objective. It does, however, highlight the objective characteristics of the Day Program that were of personal relevance to this particular person.

On the other hand, struggles around power, respect, dehumanization, and particularly around tolerating negative feelings are pervasive in human life. This sort of perspective can help the student, or anyone in her shoes, to see that the issues raised by events and relationships in the Day Program are one version of common human struggles. This perspective might help the student, and all of us, move the focus beyond the failings of this particular program. Doing so allows an identification with the program personnel, no matter how much one may take issue with their way of handling the challenges of their work. From a pragmatic point of view, identifying with people one may be trying to work with, to help, or to influence helps avoid unnecessary misunderstanding and polarization. If one is trying to work against the dehumanization of patients, it helps to avoid dehumanizing the staff. Identification is key to humanization.

Another student dove right into the issue of identification and (de)humanization by referring to a comic film in which a scatterbrained psychiatrist is running around saying, "Who is the patient? Who is the patient?" Everyone laughed. It seemed that the film had succeeded in getting people to recognize that mental health workers and their patients can share a degree of "craziness." The discussion quickly turned, however, to the difficulty telling who was the patient when many family members accompanied the patient to the hospital. At some point, a student alluded to a situation in which there were a number of interns sitting in a corner of a room with patients and family members and it seemed, at least for the moment, that any of them might have been a patient. I pointed out that it was true that any of them *might* have been a patient, and might someday indeed be a patient. Earlier in the day, several students had commented that the focus on diagnosis had seemed to objectify or dehumanize the patients. At this point, I could point out that the need to make it quite clear who the patient was, by labeling through diagnosis, had a function in helping the diagnostician disavow patient status. Thus, the misidentification and dehumanization.

## Giving and Taking in Community-Based Work

Community-based clinical work often involves no fee paid by the patient. The worker is often on salary. The project is often funded by a government agency or foundation grant. Private sector clinical work is often "fee for service," whereby the therapist provides a service in exchange for which the patient pays a fee. Community-based work provides an opportunity to notice the way private therapy involves an exchange, a commodification of the "service," a valuation of the service in monetary terms. What happens when this familiar context is absent?

Consider the following scenario: students in a class in Delhi were asked to break with the usual pattern of noncommunication between the students, faculty, construction workers, security guards, and housekeeping staff around the university buildings. The students and faculty were to initiate conversations with people whom they usually ignore and who usually ignore them.

I went out with two students and approached a group of construction workers. We encountered a family consisting of a father, mother, two sons, the father's brother and his wife, and their baby. One of the students began talking with the two boys, and the other student initiated an interaction with the baby. The mothers were working, carrying bowls of dirt on their heads, occasionally stopping to listen in, observe, participate, and facilitate the conversations. They seemed to look to the men to give a sign of approval. The men indeed seemed to approve as one of the men engaged us in conversation, told us about their village, their lives there, and finally offered us a cup of tea.

This offer posed a dilemma. We quickly thanked the man for the offer, but declined the tea. I felt uneasy that these people who made so little money would put out Rs. 30, perhaps a third of a day's wages, to buy us tea. Yet, the gesture was clearly generous; it seemed, in cultural context, arguably rude to turn it down. It seemed ungracious of us to refuse, perhaps condescending to consider that they could not afford it. The man had told us that the family owned ten acres back in their village, a not inconsiderable plot of land. I had secretly worried about cleanliness. Would the cup of tea make me sick? There was a fear of contamination that seemed unwarranted rationally. Logically, the fear seemed more a reflection of prejudice than a rational concern.

In the class, the discussion of this incident led to a consideration of the basis of untouchability, notions of purity, and so on. Then we moved on to think about the fact that this interaction did not involve money. Did the workers welcome our interest, or find it an intrusion? I told the students that although services in the private sector are often valued in terms of the monetary payment received, I place value on the act of recognizing another person's experience. It seemed that although there was some initial wariness, the man's engagement with us seemed to indicate that he valued our interest in him and his family. Indeed, when we first tried to leave, one of the women said, "Stay longer, no one ever talks to us." Perhaps, if the family felt there was value to our interest in them, the offer of tea was meant to give us something back. This interpretation would fit with an exchange model of the interaction.

A student in the class noted, however, that in Indian and many other cultures, there is a value placed on taking care of guests; this valuation of generosity toward guests seemed unrelated to an exchange model. The guest was to be treated generously regardless of whether the guest contributed anything to the host. At this point, it occurred to me that the discussion of community-based clinical work outside the fee for service model offered a space in which exchange, especially monetary exchange, was suspended.

## Primary and Secondary Prevention Mental Health Programs: Psychoanalytically Informed Community Intervention

Psychoanalytic engagement with the community can take four forms, broadly speaking. The first is a psychoanalytically informed intervention at a broad community level. Second is consultation and coordination with community-based agencies. Third is intervention with a group of people identified as "at risk," and the fourth is psychoanalytic clinical work with identified patients, occurring out of the office, in a community-based context, such as a school, hospital, community center, or another out-of-office setting. The first two forms of intervention might be understood using Arthur Kleinman's (1991) categories of preventive work; first is primary prevention (prevention before a disorder develops) in relation to individual pathology. The second is secondary prevention, meaning that a disorder has not yet developed, but is thought likely to develop. The third is tertiary prevention (i.e., intervention after the pathology or disorder has become manifest on the individual level).

There are some programs that, while not explicitly addressing mental health issues, nonetheless serve a secondary preventive function. One such is the Neighborhood Story Project (www.neighborhoodstoryproject.org): this project, founded in 2004 and based in New Orleans, Louisiana, is a series of books by residents of various communities in New Orleans documenting the conditions of their lives, as well as critical and traumatic events. Among the books in the series are five books written by students at a high school in New Orleans "investigating their worlds" in "collaborative ethnography" (www.neighborhoodstoryproject.org/about). One book describes life in some of the city's public housing projects as they were being torn down (Bolding, 2005). Another book describes and documents life in one of the ongoing public housing projects (Nelson, 2005). Many of the book's authors are adolescents. The books contain reflections by the authors, interviews by and with community residents, and photography. They document the fabric of daily life in the author's community, the ordinary stresses and forms of resilience, community support and caretaking, the role of illegal drugs, their consumption and sale, the gangs, and the murders. In the tradition of oral history, this project fosters community-based reflection on communal and individual lives. The project generates appreciation of the assets and strengths of communities, which are often devalued and pathologized in the media and isolated from "mainstream" society. The project provides a vehicle for the processing of losses, often through murder, various forms of trauma, as well as neglect by the larger society.

Other examples of projects that serve secondary prevention functions in the realm of mental health are found in the work of Ricardo Ainslie (1995, 1999, 2002–2006, 2004, 2006, 2007, 2013a, 2013b). Although a psychoanalyst himself, Ainslie's work is more broadly community focused in a way that builds psychic strength and resilience capacity on a community-wide basis. Ainslie's (1995) first book, *No Dancin' in Anson*, was a study of the small, West Texas community of Anson. Having been settled by white Southern Baptists and members of the Church of Christ, Anson had a law on the books prohibiting dancing in the city limits. This situation was destabilized as people of Mexican ancestry, who had been prohibited from living in the town before the Civil Rights era, had moved in. They, along with recently arrived white people who were not members of the fundamentalist churches, wanted to dance. Here was a look at the process of change in the political dynamics of the United States around race on a microcosmic level. Ainslie noted: "In Texas, Mexican ancestry people were governed by the same Jim Crow laws that governed lives of African-Americans in the American South" (Ainslie, personal communication, August 27, 2013). As this situation changed following the Civil Rights movement, the role that people of Mexican ancestry could play in the community, in relation to white people, began to change. The book provided a fine-grained look at the resulting human dynamics similar to the fine-grained look at human interaction on an individual and dyadic level that occurs in the psychotherapy consulting room.

Ainslie's interest in social change continued with his retrospective study of the desegregation process in Hempstead, Texas (Ainslie, 1999). Using film as his medium, he interviewed people who had experienced this time of fundamental social change in the context of deeply entrenched racial suspicion and hatred. Ainslie began with the premise that the disruption of the centuries-old segregation of the races had been a trauma, largely unresolved, for this small town. His thinking was informed by psychoanalytic notions that the resolution or processing of trauma occurs through psychic representation and symbolization. Accordingly, he interviewed Hempstead residents, black and white, about their memories, thoughts, and feelings about the desegregation process. He filmed some of these interviews, creating a documentary, *Crossover: A Study of Desegregation.* With the film, a representation of the experience of desegregation had been constructed in the form of an oral history, but its integration into the community psyche had yet to be accomplished.

The trauma that Ainslie's work highlighted, somewhat unexpectedly, was the loss of the black school, the Sam Schwarz School. In the dominant narrative among white people, the desegregation process was intended to benefit black people in the United States. From a more enlightened point of view, perhaps, desegregation was intended to benefit all United States citizens, black and white, bringing people and cultures together. Ainslie's closer look revealed that the black community in Hempstead had actually lost a great deal with desegregation. With the closing of the Sam Schwarz School, many black teachers had lost their jobs. The achievements of students were lost to community memory in many cases, concretized in the disappearance of trophies and awards earned by students. The white community failed to register the price paid within the black community by the loss of the Sam Schwarz School. The school was torn down and, adding insult to injury, a school for students on in-school suspension was constructed on the site of the school into which many black students were tracked (i.e., resegregated).

In an effort to represent and process this loss to the black community, as well as to the larger community of Hempstead, Ainslie formed a committee to plan an event, "The Sam Schwarz Reunion and Retrospective." In Ainslie's words,

> Sam Schwarz teachers, administrators, and alumni were recognized, and the choir sang the school's song. In an especially meaningful gesture, the school set up two permanent display cases in its offices at the site of the original school. The in-school suspension program had by now been moved elsewhere; the school district had moved its offices to the site, which retained its name, "Sam Schwarz campus." Alumni had donated photographs and memorabilia that were to be on permanent display. My task was to describe the era of school desegregation as a collective trauma drawing from the dozens of interviews my students and I had done regarding the demise of the Sam Schwarz school.
>
> (Ainslie, 2013b, p. 150)

Several highly accomplished alumni spoke at the event, including a university dean, a cardiac surgeon, and the first black pediatric surgeon in the state of Texas. Ainslie notes that the film "became a training tool in a National Endowment for the Humanities collaboration with Humanities Texas and the association of historically African-American colleges in Texas, training black students to go back to their communities and conduct oral histories of the experience of school desegregation in their communities" (Ainslie, personal communication, August 27, 2013). Thus, the film gave people around Texas the opportunity to reflect from a distance in time on a process that had been extremely conflictual and all-consuming while it was occurring.

In this way, as a community psychoanalyst, Ainslie orchestrated a community intervention, guided by psychoanalytically derived notions that putting traumatic experience into words and other symbols and representations has a healing effect. As it was, the experience of school desegregation had been traumatic, in the sense of being overwhelming and unprocessable for both black and white communities in Hempstead. For black people, there had been a loss, a dispossession, of a site for community life, struggle, and achievement, echoing the loss of place and identity that had occurred with slavery. For white people, there had been an unthinking dehumanization of fellow human beings such that they could be robbed of key elements of their identity as if nothing had happened. Again, echoes of slavery. For whites, the trauma was an unprocessable, undischargeable load of guilt, the same sort of guilt that had to be denied by the ongoing dehumanization of blacks so that it would seem to make no difference that they were objectified. Ainslie's contribution was to represent what had happened in words, images, and restored memories so that an aborted process of community-wide healing could be restarted.

In Anson, Ainslie was looking at how people and groups manage to adapt and change when caught up in social-historical evolution. As in an individual life, there were forces opposing change, as well as circumstances and internal forces requiring and favoring change. The forces opposing change were rooted in beliefs in God-given moral standards and prohibitions around sex, a sort of socially shared superego. The forces for change were not only circumstantial (the arrival of people of Mexican origin and like-minded white people), but also the very pleasure in dancing which had set off religiously based repression. Additionally, there was what one might call a social ego function seeking integration, evolution, and development. Such an evolution was occurring in Hempstead, as well, but this time in the context of a history of vicious circles of hatred and violence.

Another of Ainslie's projects was a study of the aftermath of the murder of James Bird in Jasper, Texas (Ainslie, 2004). In 1998, Bird, a black man, was picked up by Bill King, Russell Brewer, and Shawn Berry late one night as he walked home and dragged to his death behind a pickup truck. The three white men were quickly arrested; King was tried first, convicted, and is now on death row. Bill King was the first white man convicted of murder and sentenced to death for killing a black man in Texas since the Reconstruction. Brewer was later also convicted and sentenced to death, while Berry was convicted and sentenced to life imprisonment.

In the wake of Bird's murder, the situation in Jasper quickly became volatile; the town became a magnet for potentially violent white and black groups, from the Ku Klux Klan to the Black Panthers. Further violence could so easily have been sparked, violence that would have raged out of control until it exhausted itself with many people dead and injured. Ainslie and his students explored the process within the town by which violence was defused, a process in which an interracial group of clergy successfully played a containing role. In psychoanalytic language, Ainslie was studying the process of impulse control and containing (Bion, 1988) in a social context. The town, its white and black citizens, as a group was called upon to come to terms with an unthinkable act, an outburst of racial violence, echoing countless lynchings and other acts of sadistic violence against black people that had left a reservoir of rage. Ainslie (2004) also wrote a biography of Bill King in which he studied the events in his life leading up to the murder.

Ainslie's interest in social chaos and social containment continued with his study of the violence in Juarez, Mexico (Ainslie, 2013a). During the last decade, Juarez had become a battle ground for warring drug cartels. The police were largely in the employ of the cartels, and government officials who tried to take action against them were often gunned down in broad daylight in the center of the city. An exception was Mayor Jose Reyes Ferriz, who lived in a bank vault-like structure within his home. Ainslie's book gives a vivid picture of a man at the epicenter of a city in disorder who survives long enough for the national government and the army to begin to restore some degree of rule of law. Reyes Ferriz continued as mayor until October 2010, but according to Ainslie,

> the violence continued to be out of control for another 15 months or so. I think the Juarez story is really one of collective trauma. Everyone in this city of 1.3 million people was directly affected by the violence that turned Juarez into the most violent city in the Americas (some say the world). Over 7,000 people were killed in the city over the course of Reyes-Ferriz' three-year term. One important argument in the book is that the violence not only reflected the war between the two cartels but also was symptomatic of the breakdown of the social fabric of the city.
>
> (Ainslie, personal communication, August 27, 2013)

When I teach courses in race, social class, and culture, there is from time to time a critique that the course is "too political" or "too theoretical," sometimes "not clinical enough." The latter critique is valid, in my view, if class discussion stays at too abstract a level without considering the implications on the ground of the way we think and organize our experience. Sometimes, however, the critique that the discussion is too "political" reflects a belief that it is possible to separate the way political power is organized in society from human feelings and interactions. I am reminded of an interview with Otto Kernberg (Kernberg, 1995, p. 343) in which I asked him whether he thought the Oedipus complex was a function of patriarchal society. He replied, "All the politically correct questions!" I suggest that if I had not asked this question, we still would have been leaving in political considerations. That is, power structures operate invisibly as people are socialized to take them for granted and to regard them as reflecting some sort of law of nature. We take political positions by failing to take explicitly political positions. This proposition corresponds to the relational psychoanalytic idea that the analyst is always interacting with the patient, even when silent. Silence, as we all know, inevitably has some sort of impact on one's interlocutor, sometimes a very powerful impact. Yet, some analysts continue to believe that it is possible to avoid "influencing the transference."

Ainslie's work documents the value of transcendence of the boundaries between the clinical and the political. I suggest that part of the exclusivity of psychoanalysis relates to its splendid isolation in the consulting room. To be more community based, psychoanalysis needs to be more *of* the community. Not only in the sense that psychoanalytic understanding is relevant to understanding social dynamics on a large scale, but that psychoanalysis should be thought to include understandings and interventions that occur in the world at large. In this sense, I think it is not helpful to term psychoanalytic consideration of the arts and politics "applied psychoanalysis." This implies that there is a form of psychoanalysis that is not applied. How can analysts hope to be considered relevant to, and by, the world we live in with that belief intact? An insistence on defining psychoanalysis in a way that excludes or diminishes the relevance of the external world results in a widespread perception of the field as irrelevant to crucial public concerns. Kumar (2012) made this point in a dramatic fashion by investigating the way in which the word "poverty" appeared in psychoanalytic literature. She found a variety of uses, the great majority of which referred to mental poverty, a poverty of mental life, for example. Kumar points out that one fifth of the world's population is living in "absolute poverty" (i.e., without the bare minimum of material resources). For psychoanalysis to ignore the poor and poverty is to forfeit its opportunity to acknowledge and contribute to the understanding of peoples' inattention to an overwhelmingly important source of human suffering. Kumar points out that the psychoanalytic aspiration to address resistance to the awareness of suffering is undermined by this unreflected-upon inattention to massive suffering.

Chaos, containment, regulation, and control: these are concepts that apply on both the individual and social levels. There is a specifically psychoanalytic way of thinking about how unthinkable chaos becomes transformed into experience that can be processed, thought about, and contained. There is also a specifically psychoanalytic praxis for addressing chaos, the unthinkable. When psychoanalysis is thought about in strictly intrapsychic terms, the whole realm of social chaos and containment is ruled out of the psychoanalytic domain. We wonder why psychoanalysis is considered irrelevant in and to the world we live.

But when psychoanalysis is considered to be relevant on all levels from the individual intrapsychic to the macrocosmic social level, its relevance is enhanced. Further, encompassing a variety of levels in this way opens up an opportunity for psychoanalysis to develop a systemic point of view in which the individual, the dyadic, and the small and large group social levels are linked. Ainslie's work opens up just such an opportunity.

Opportunities are opened up to link, theoretically, the various levels from the individual to the social and for rethinking praxis (i.e., for considering new ways psychoanalysis can be deployed in the world, and not just in the consulting room). Ainslie's methods include ethnography (*No Dancin' in Anson*, 1995), documentary film (*Crossover: A Study of Desegregation*, 1999, *Looking North: Mexican Images of Immigration*, 2006, and *Ya Basta*, 2007, a study of a wave of kidnappings in Mexico), and photography (*Jasper, Texas: The Healing of a Community in Crisis*), as well as books including the biographical study of Bill King (Ainslie, 2004), and the work in Juarez, Mexico (Ainslie, 2013a).

Psychoanalysts and psychotherapists have worked on a number of secondary prevention projects with more explicit aims to foster mental health. Some recent examples include an outreach program to Iraq War veterans, SOFAR (Darwin, 2012), interventions targeting former child soldiers in Angola (Bragin, 2004), Sklarew, Handel, and Ley's (2012) RECOVER program that reaches out to people arriving at the Washington, D.C. morgue to identify loved ones who were lost under traumatic circumstances, and Marans' (2004) partnership between the Yale Child Study Center and the New Haven Police. Some of these projects make highly creative use of psychoanalytic ways of thinking. For example, keeping in mind Klein's (1975) concept of reparation as important in the processing and integration of destructiveness, Bragin (2004) had former child soldiers accompany and protect those carrying medicine and food to people in need after the war ended. Bragin (2004) comments, "In this way they could freely fantasize violence while protecting others from it and being protected themselves; at the same time, they could perform reparative activity to address their terrifying unconscious guilt" (p. 181).

A psychoanalytically guided community intervention was carried out and described by Twemlow and Wilkinson (2004) and Twemlow (2013). Twemlow undertook a "Healthy Community Initiative" (HCI) in Topeka, Kansas. The "presenting problem" was a breakdown in the relationship between the mayor and the City Council. This breakdown was having a demoralizing effect on the city. There was a general sense that no one was in charge as crime rates rose to high levels in a context of extreme racial and ethnic divisiveness. Twemlow, a member of the faculty at the nearby Menninger Institute, was asked by the mayor, with the grudging assent of the City Council, to intervene.

Twemlow and Wilkinson's (2004) approach was guided by the principles of "stabilizing systems and healthy capacities" (p. 110). These values were seen as community parallels to individual ego functions. A committee was put together called the Healthy Community Committee that included community members who were considered to have a commitment to a stable community. The four systems that were thought to be crucial to community stabilization included criminal justice and law enforcement, the religious community, education, and social services. Politicians and business people were not included because of their commitment to competitive and short-term gain, rather than process-oriented approaches to decision making. Notably, the economic system was not one of the systems targeted for stabilization. Twemlow believed that economic development would follow from stabilization of the four target systems. HCI's premise was that in the absence of stability, people are prone to passivity, indifference, or demandingness. Representatives from all the four target systems met together, with a deliberately slow-paced, informal style. The expectation was that people from one system would see the blind spots of another (i.e., would serve a function parallel to that of an individual therapist). As in a therapeutic interaction, it was thought that solutions built on trust and understanding would be more durable than those built on mutual material advantage. Credit for progress made would go to those actively involved in change, in a process of HCI's disengagement from the community parallel to the termination phase of individual therapy. Some of the principles that guided the HCI project included the importance of taking time to develop a collaborative process in group meetings, diagnosing competitive as opposed to collaborative mindsets in community leaders, and the importance of shared personal experience. This last principle led, for example, to group visits to distressed, high crime, "at risk" and "intensive care" communities. It was expected and hoped that HCI members from more affluent neighborhoods would see and experience aspects of community life that had previously been unknown to them. In a remark reminiscent of Ainslie's about white ignorance and indifference about the fate of the Sam Schwarz School, Twemlow notes: "our collective self-realization that we had been so blind to the plight of our fellow Topekans. Our blindness made us complicit" (Twemlow & Wilkinson, 2004, pp. 122–123). And, highlighting the contribution of psychoanalytic thinking, "We had learned a difficult lesson about countertransference, denial, and projection when we had to acknowledge the degree to which we had overlooked the problems in the At Risk and Intensive Care Communities" (p. 123). Citing an intersubjective approach to psychoanalysis, Twemlow cultivated an attitude that there were no objective experts, only participants in a group consciousness-raising project that would enhance community-wide collaboration. A review of the project after eighteen months highlighted goals of supporting successful community-based initiatives, a focus on the welfare of children, the development of neighborhood organizations, mobilizing community spirit, and development of a strong community self-image. This last goal led to a community theater performance in which a community reviewed aspects of its own history, a project strikingly similar to Ainslie's "Sam Schwarz Reunion and Retrospective."

As Twemlow reviewed the history of the project itself, he noted that the mayor who had initiated and supported it was defeated in an extremely contentious campaign, followed by his own departure from Topeka. The HCI group became divided between those who became demoralized, and those who wanted to carry forward the spirit of the group. As in a psychoanalytic therapy, "working through" over and over is to be expected, with the process marked by ongoing struggle with, and understanding of, anxiety, defense, blind spots, and enactments. Perhaps the marginalization of the business and political communities led to a blind spot around competition, ruthlessness, and greed that eventually returned from repression to demand its due. A key value of a psychoanalytic clinical perspective is the expectation it provides that blind spots and enactments are continuous; the unconscious continually regenerates itself. The Healthy Community Initiative built on collaboration as a value at the expense of competing values that could not be denied. The next step might be, or might have been, to do some soul searching and consciousness raising, and to try to include those aspects of the community that had been marginalized.

## Pitfalls of Community Mental Health Programs Without Consideration of Race, Social Class, and Culture

It is not enough simply to serve the underserved. Surely, neglect of economically disadvantaged communities by mental health professionals is one reflection of prejudice based on race, class, and culture. In the absence of ongoing critical reflection on one's interactions with people across these socioeconomic divides, however, provision of more mental health services by members of economically and politically privileged groups can mean more unwitting enactments of prejudicial and demeaning assumptions about the people served in economically and politically underprivileged communities. This problem can take one or more of the following forms:

1. The uncritical application of linear and normative developmental models.
2. A failure to note how white, mainstream culture is a particular vantage point from which to view and make judgments about nonmainstream cultural groups and people.
3. Failure to note that economically advantaged and disadvantaged communities all have strengths and weaknesses. An unreflective assumption is that economic disadvantage necessarily entails inadequacies in child rearing, for example, with little awareness of the strengths and resiliencies in economically disadvantaged communities, along with the weaknesses and liabilities that may accompany economic advantage.

The problem of linear developmental models is fundamental to many of the manifold forms that prejudice can take. Linear developmental models, whether applied to individuals or groups of people, create hierarchies of maturity and immaturity, of high and low levels of functioning. When these hierarchies are taken as objectively and universally valid (i.e., as transcending culturally specific value systems), they can seem to give a scientific stamp of approval to culturally prejudicial judgments about people and groups of people. One example includes the assumptions that once underlay separation-individuation theory (Mahler, Pine, & Bergman, 1975). A linear sequence was set up with the immature end characterized as "autistic" or "symbiotic," the mature end characterized by "separation" and "individuation." One problem here was that the early forms of connection were characterized by complete undifferentiation ("autistic") or parasitism ("symbiotic"). Very quickly, some observers of children (Stern, 1985) noted that infants in the first days of life showed evidence of differentiation of self and others. Over time, the bias in favor of differentiation was modified as interest increased in attachment theory (Bowlby, 1969; Ainsworth, Blehar, Waters, & Walls, 1978; Main & Hesse, 1990). Attachment theory recognizes that attachment to caregivers is universal, growth promoting, and essential to life. The emphasis among researchers and theorists shifted away from a progression toward increasing differentiation, toward a recognition that attachment is present at all points in development, but taking different forms at different times and in different circumstances, including various cultural circumstances. The separation-individuation model assumed, or reinforced, several interrelated assumptions. It was assumed that in normal development, there is a progression from autism and symbiosis to differentiation and individuation, the early stages being immature. In a normative developmental framework, immaturity that lasts beyond its appropriate stage comes to imply pathology, as do the very words autistic and symbiotic. The later stages of differentiation and individuation are mature (i.e., healthy). The individualistic value system that is prominent and widespread in Western culture is reflected in this normative developmental framework. The colonial assumption that cultures with communal value systems (i.e., where the welfare of the community is put ahead of, or alongside of, the welfare of the individual) are inferior is reinforced (see Brickman, 2003, for a penetrating discussion of how colonial value systems are built in to psychoanalytic theories).

Attachment theories are normative, but not linear. Attachment is assumed to be universal; the theory addresses different attachment *styles*. Attachment to caregivers and others *per se* is not pathologized as autistic or symbiotic; there are healthy (i.e., secure) and unhealthy (i.e., insecure) ways of being attached. The normative biases are reflected in the way healthy and unhealthy ways of being are defined. For example, emotion that is regulated and modulated in a certain way is privileged. Avoidant and clingy, or inconsistent, ways of being with others are pathologized as "insecure" or "disorganized." Attachment theory's normative assumptions, however, do not rest on a linear progression from insecure to secure. Rather, they rest on judgments about healthy and unhealthy ways of interacting with significant other people. Health and pathology are located *between* people rather than *within* people, though the residue of healthy and unhealthy interactions can persist as individual health and pathology.

Attachment theory's normative biases, too, have a cultural basis. Ainsworth's original studies (Ainsworth, 1963, 1967) were conducted in Uganda, so she had some basis for a cross-cultural comparison. Researchers have found that avoidant attachment styles are relatively common in Northern European countries such as Germany and Scandinavia (Grossmann, Grossmann, Spangler, Suess, & Unzner, 1985). It is easy to imagine that emotional expression that qualifies as "regulated" might differ from Southern to Northern European countries, or between Latin America and North America. In a different cultural framework, the issue might not be regulation at all; some other aspect of emotional expression or behavior might be the focus. In short, normative theories, whether based on linear developmental progressions or not, reflect culturally based value systems. If words such as "normal," "healthy," and "optimal" are not set in the context of the cultural value systems that underlie them, they tend to reflect and reinforce a sense that a certain set of norms are objectively and universally valid. For example, consider the following sentence from a description of an exemplary community-based police-mental health partnership (Marans, 2004). "To help children and their families return to the optimal paths of development and functioning, CD-CP (Child Development-Community Policing) partners continuously attempt to learn more about the implications of our respective interventions" (p. 233). From the point of view being developed here, one important way of learning about the implications of one's interventions would be to reflect on the cultural assumptions contained in one's notions of what constitutes "optimal paths of development and functioning," and how these interact with the value systems of those whom one is helping.

Difference, organized into norms and hierarchies, tends to slide into deviance and deficit. Here is the reason why studies of community-based mental health programs need to consider race, social class, ethnicity, and culture, along with gender and sexual orientation. More specifically, consideration of differences along these dimensions are a precondition for reflectiveness on one's own biases and prejudices so that one can avoid the devaluation and pathologization of people who are different from oneself, especially given that such prejudices are rampant in the culture that surrounds us.

In order to develop a reflective attitude about one's own racial, class, and cultural prejudices, however, one must develop a degree of reflectiveness about one's own cultural location. One cannot take for granted one's own point of view, the location from which one views others who are differently situated. The process of becoming aware of one's own prejudices is strikingly similar to the psychoanalytic process of becoming aware of one's blind spots as a person. In this respect, psychoanalysis offers a model of how to become aware of oneself in a cultural sense so as to be able to see others while being increasingly aware of the cultural lenses one is wearing. The psychoanalytic idea of the unconscious implies that the process is never ending. Blind spots keep popping up. No sooner does one become aware of one blind spot than another appears, usually from an unexpected quarter. The unconscious regenerates itself no matter how much one has managed to raise one's consciousness. There is always more to know, including more of oneself and one's culturally shaped expectations and norms.

The process of locating oneself in terms of race, social class, and culture is a special challenge for those who consider themselves white in the United States, or for any others who consider their own culture the standard, the unremarkable norm, in the context in which they live. Consider the following from a chapter about a school-based mourning project (Sklarew, Krupnick, Ward-Wimmer, & Napoli, 2002):

> Minimal clinical contact with lower class white families led to the question of how race and social class interact to influence the ability to mourn effectively. One of us (B.S.) approached this issue with the late Charles Pinderhughes (personal communication, 1995), one of the first African-American psychoanalysts. Pinderhughes elaborated that over thousands of years, African cultures had developed rituals around mourning and loss. Fewer than 150 years ago, during slavery, not only were families dissolved, but efforts to annihilate these millennia-old traditions forced African-Americans to start anew.
>
> (p. 197)

The authors begin by recognizing that, because of lack of clinical contact, they have no data about the mourning process in children of lower class white families. They recognize that any conclusions they draw from their presumably homogenous African-American sample would apply only to this racial group. In my view, however, the problem is not only that they have no white subjects, but also that the researchers themselves are, presumably, entirely white. They do not explicitly identify themselves as white, or in fact as belonging to any racial group. We cannot locate their racially inflected perspective on their racially homogenous group of subjects, which makes their perspective invisible, but "white" in the sense of being unmarked. We can infer that the researchers are white, or at least not African-American, from the fact that they approached an outside African-American analyst for his perspective on the racial issue. One wonders why they identify him as eminent ("one of the first African-American analysts"). If the point is to establish his authority about racial issues, one wonders why a less eminent African-American analyst, or an African-American analyst not identified by eminence, or even an African-American who was not an analyst, could not have provided the needed perspective. And what was that needed perspective? If one wants information about how white people mourn, if not lower class white people, one might ask a white person, or white people. (I am setting aside for the moment the issue of generalization.) In one respect, however, I think asking a black person for his observations is useful, in that the cross-racial perspective is important, especially in cases where one's own perspective is invisible to oneself. As a rule, one's own perspective tends to be invisible to oneself, often usefully manifest only in interaction with another person or people. That is why we need someone else to be our therapist. In the case of white people, whose perspective is regarded as the standard of objectivity in the culture, one's perspective is doubly invisible. A nonwhite person's observations about white people are thus doubly useful, though not to be substituted for the self-observations of white people.

The observations of Charles Pinderhughes, however, are about black people, or at least so it seems on the surface. If one wants to learn about how lower class white people mourn, of what use is it to learn that there were millennia-old traditions around mourning and loss in Africa? That, in fact, these traditions along with most other African traditions were stripped from Africans when they became slaves in North America? Stated this way, one becomes aware of learning *something* about white people from Charles Pinderhughes: white people felt it necessary to strip African slaves of their traditions. What does this fact have to do with mourning and loss among white people? What do I lose when I take something away from you? Here, one can find a profound observation about race in what Pinderhughes said in the context of this interaction with Sklarew. White people lost something of themselves when they annihilated the traditions of the Africans among them. What was so threatening to white people about the traditions, indeed the identities, of the Africans they had enslaved? I propose the following: one cannot enslave people who have identities (i.e., humanity like one's own). One can only enslave them if they are reduced to nonhuman property. What white people lost was their humanity. Racism was the way that white people dealt with, and deal with, that loss. Such dynamics of dehumanization of others as a way of justifying inhumane treatment of them has been recognized and studied empirically by Bandura (1990) and Castano and Giner-Sorolla (2006), among others. White racism, one might say, is a substitute for, a defense against, mourning.

## Whiteness, Hierarchy, and Linear Developmental Models

Social structures in which one group's culture, cultural norms, and point of view are regarded as standard tend to lead to other, nonmainstream cultures being regarded as deviant and inferior. The ability of a group to regard its own culture as standard arises from, and perpetuates, its dominance in terms of political, economic, and military power. The hierarchy of groups and cultures originates in the perspective of the dominant group, although it is also subject to being internalized by members of nondominant groups. Alternatively, when there is cultural diversity, one could imagine a situation in which difference is acknowledged without there being a superior standard category. In the United States, in particular, there is a value placed on equality of people and peoples creating a conflict with de facto hierarchy of people and cultures. One way this conflict can be resolved is through the denial on the part of members of the dominant group of the ways in which members of subordinate groups are devalued. Such devaluation can occur without the conscious awareness of all parties, although it is likely to be especially invisible to members of the dominant group for whom the conflict between professed values and the reality of hierarchy is likely to be especially salient.

One interesting, special case is the way that some immigrant groups to the United States seek to attain a status as "white" by devaluing and denigrating other people regarded as nonwhite. Ignatiev (1993) wrote of "How the Irish became White" after initially identifying with the slaves as fellow oppressed people. Some Irish sought the benefits of whiteness by turning in a racist direction during the Draft Riots in New York during the 1860s. This story has been repeated in the United States many times, with the newest immigrant group at the time (Italians, Jews, Latinos) regarded as non-white until anti-black racism sometimes serves to establish their white credentials, with the privileges thereto associated, by demonstrating that someone else is even darker than they are. At this moment, in the context of globalization, some immigrants in the United States seek to establish a privileged status for their group by devaluing or, worse, rendering invisible, economically poor African-Americans. Consider the following narrative by Kishore Mahbubani (2013, p. 352), the dean of Lee Kuan Yew School of Public Policy at the National University of Singapore. He writes, "America welcomes immigrants from all over the globe, offers them a level playing field, and encourages them to test themselves against world class competition . . . and who has come out ahead in this unparalleled global free-for-all? Indians. Their per capita income now ranks as the highest of any ethnic group in the States." The "level" playing field Mahbubani refers to leaves out any references to how the playing field is tilted against the descendants of slaves (not to say that many descendants of slaves have not overcome the disadvantages of inferior education and prejudice) and the fact that those Indians who manage to emigrate from India are mostly from very privileged backgrounds. Mahbubani also leaves out any reference to restrictive immigration quotas in the United States.

This denial of devaluation even finds its way into efforts to help members of disadvantaged and devalued communities in the United States. In fact, helpers might be especially prone to devaluation of members of subordinate communities because of the blatant conflict with their professed desire to counter the effects of disadvantage, subordination, and devaluation. Following are some cases in point from efforts to bring the benefits of community mental health to underserved communities.

Osofsky and Osofsky (2004) describe the "Violence Intervention Program" in New Orleans, conducted by Louisiana State University's Department of Psychiatry. Children were referred who had been exposed to the violence that was epidemic in inner-city New Orleans, as well as elsewhere around the United States at the time. In addition to describing the nature of their clinical program, Osofsky and Osofsky make some generalizations about children who are exposed to violence, describing the children with whom they are concerned as "living in inner city environments" (p. 240), "where sustained and unremitting actual trauma, including physical and sexual abuse, neglect, and violence occur with some regularity" (p. 241). These conditions of life, according to Osofsky and Osofsky, "suggest negative behavioral and affective outcomes that likely affect the children's psychic structure" (p. 241). "These children" (note the generalization) display a range of problem behaviors that include impulsive and acting out behaviors rather than verbalization, verbal and physical aggression, and little frustration tolerance or future orientation. In such children, object relations are primitive, reflecting at best ambivalent interactions with others. "Such children" (again the generalization) "lack the ability for basic trust. . . . Their defenses are rigid and archaic, interfering with adaptive functioning" (p. 241).

The generalizations in the above statement are quite indefinite with respect to which children are being portrayed as having substandard development. Exposure to violence is grouped together with abuse and neglect. There is not a systematic disclosure of the social class, race, or ethnicity of the children beyond the occasional mention of poverty. Clearly, the authors are not writing about all children who are exposed to violence. They are not talking about children who were exposed to the violence of mass shootings in schools, for example, who are likely to be from economically privileged environments and white. One presumes that in New Orleans in the early 1990s, Osofsky and Osofsky were referring to economically poor black children, but the lack of specificity, along with the generalizations about the sequelae for psychological functioning, leave some confusion as to who exactly is at risk for deficient psychological development. Left out of the equations being made are children from white and/or economically privileged families who are sexually and physically abused and/or exposed to domestic violence. Such cases, especially those of lower socioeconomic status, may be systematically underrecognized (Laskey et al., 2012), creating a potentially misleading correlation between socioeconomic status, race, trauma of various kinds, and deficient psychological development. Even if research were to provide evidence that supports correlations between any or all of these variables, correlation does not establish causation. Without some understanding of the dynamics behind an association between low socioeconomic status, or race, and child abuse, for example, one is left only with stereotypes. Racial, ethnic, and socioeconomic categories are lumped together under the heading "inner city." This category is then linked to deficient, abusive, neglectful parenting, then to deficient psychological development. All these linkages are made without consideration of any potential causal pathways. Under these conditions, there is considerable scope for reinforcement of pernicious and prejudicial stereotypes. In short, there is a need in studies of the kind that Osofsky and Osofsky, among many others, report of community-based interventions to include an in-depth consideration of the dynamics of social class, race, and ethnicity.

The potential to reinforce prejudicial stereotypes is enhanced when a linear developmental model is used to define normal and abnormal, or deficient, psychological development and functioning. In Osofsky and Osofsky's (2004) article, psychoanalysis provides such a model. Consider the following statement from their article (p. 243):

> Psychoanalysis has been described as more than therapy. It is a method for learning about the mind, and also as a theory, a way of understanding the processes of normal, everyday mental functioning through the stages of normal development from infancy to old age.

The word "normal" in this, or any, context is very tricky. On one hand, one would have to agree that it is "normal" for a child to walk or talk sometime before the second birthday. On the other hand, there are behaviors under this category that are mostly, or purely, the norm in a particular cultural context, and not in another. An example is affect regulation. It is perhaps easy to agree that affect must be regulated in some way, but one culture's dyscontrol is another culture's usual form of expressiveness, while one culture's usual form of emotional expressiveness is inhibited and stiff by another standard. One sort of problem occurs when behavior beyond the usual becomes "abnormal" in the sense of pathological (in a medical-model context). Another sort of problem emerges when the notions of normal and abnormal or pathological are extended to include the environment. That is, when it is thought that normal behavior or development depends on a "facilitating environment" (Winnicott, 1971), then environments, including caretakers, can be classified into "normal" and "abnormal" or "pathological" environments. One can see this development in Osofsky and Osofsky's (2004) article, as the development of "normal" everyday mental functioning as referred to above is said to depend on a normal parenting environment:

> Without necessary sensitivity to the developmental and emotional needs of the child, there may be a derailment of the normal developmental process, and even a polarization of affect, "the splitting of affect" that is characteristic of borderline pathology.
>
> (Osofsky & Osofsky, 2004, p. 244)

One can see in this passage how the notion of "normal development," coupled with generalizations about the "inner city" and the people in it, slides into pathological stereotypes that mirror prejudicial attitudes in the culture at large.

Psychoanalysis is invoked here to prescribe not only a set of norms for the way lives should unfold over time, but also norms as to the kind of environments in which people should be raised and children reared. Because inner cities do not meet the criteria for a health-promoting environment, the people in them are thought likely not to develop normally. One finds similar negative stereotypes about inner city people in Holmes' (1995) description of work done in a preschool in a family center in North London. The socioeconomic and cultural status of the population of families in this preschool are not specified, nor is the referral system by which the families ended up sending their children to this center. Yet, it seems implicit that the families are economically disadvantaged and considered culturally deprived. Consider the following passage:

> it is necessary to appreciate the importance for these children of seeing the same person in the same room at the same time every day. This, for many of them, is the first time that they can predict what will happen, with whom, where and when, with certainty.
>
> (Holmes, 1995, p. 150)

And:

> For the first time in his life, the child is exposed to extensive language stimulation directed to him personally . . . not to a group of children, not from a television set.
>
> (Holmes, 1995, p. 152)

The stereotype here seems all the more insidious when the group to which it refers is unspecified, as if everyone would know, or the author does not want to be thought to be openly prejudiced against a particular group. She continues:

> It is essential that the teacher does not allow herself to be distracted by colleagues, visitors, telephone calls, or any other interruption . . . in the classroom the children are the focus of attention . . . if they ask a question it is

answered, if they need help it is provided . . . their favorite book is always in the same place and the routine is welcomed. For insecure children who have moved from pillar to post physically as well as emotionally, the safety of this ordered classroom becomes a haven and a relief.

(Holmes, 1995, p. 150)

In this passage, one sees not only the denigration of the home environment, but the idealization of the school environment in a way which smacks of splitting and which will likely put the children into conflict about their homes and families. The experiences in the school environment will likely fail to prepare the children for the environments, even the best of environments, in which they actually spend their lives and will continue to spend their lives.

Holmes (1995) evidences a cultural bias against life in extended families, in which the children in her preschool are evidently being raised:

It appears to be a consequence of group living that so much speech around them is irrelevant that they learn to ignore much of the language they hear, and cannot then distinguish between relevant and irrelevant speech.

(p. 152)

Left out of the equation in the examples just cited are the resiliencies people develop under stress, as well as the ways in which inner cities may provide particularly growth-promoting environments for people. More fundamentally, there is an unreflected-upon value system that creates a hierarchy of behaviors and ways of being, and a categorization of peoples based on where they show up on this hierarchy of values. Within a society, the perceived *value* of individuals and groups of people is related to where they show up on the culture's underlying hierarchically organized system of values. Prejudice and marginalization is connected with perceived failure or underdevelopment on the linearly organized dimensions arising from the culture's value system.

These value systems are not monolithic and they are always refracted through the prism of individual, familial, community, and subcommunity value systems. More fundamentally, privileged values appear in the foreground, while those that are denigrated persist in the background, unconsciously, as it were. For example, individualists, a few hermits notwithstanding, need other individualists for support and with whom to band together, even in order to oppose misguided communally oriented people. Nonetheless, consciously held value systems form a structure of ideals against which people evaluate themselves, their worth as individuals, families, and communities. The warded off, but persisting, negative values form an ever-present sense of threat that tends to be projected onto those who, denigrated, embody the negative ideals.

To take an example: the system of values in North America creates a hierarchy in which individual initiative and achievement tends to be placed above communal values. This, of course, is a value system that arises from and reinforces the capitalist economy; it is reflected in a negative attitude toward the public sector and government (except its military and police functions) and a wish to be free of government interference with private initiative. The "self" as defined in this cultural context tends to be a "masterful, bounded self" (Cushman, 1995), an individualized self rather than a communal self (Roland, 1988). Communal welfare is valued within this communal cultural context, especially when people are closely identified with the community in question. As noted above, this hierarchy of values is neither universal nor absolute.

The popularity and pervasiveness of suburbs and exurbs in North America is consistent with this loosely defined value system. Each individual family has its own private property, its own house, and its own piece of land. Municipalities are organized in a fragmented way so that the public sector, such as it is, is not very inclusive. Suburbs tend to be quite homogenous with respect to social class and race. The individualized, disconnected self that is privileged in the culture are physically reflected in the disconnected houses and private cars of the United States suburbs.

The inner city (as opposed to gentrified urban life), by contrast, features communal life. Life depends on the public sector in many ways: large public education systems, public transportation, garbage collection, and so on. Taxes are crucial for urban life. People live together in multifamily buildings. The people who tend to live in inner cities are from cultures that place a higher value on community life, on a communal self. Centers of community life, like stoops, street corners, barber shops and beauty salons, and churches, are often a more prominent feature of life in such urban contexts.

With society constructed in this way, inner cities and their inhabitants in the United States become a convenient magnet for the projections of suburban dwellers who would like to believe they have arrived at an economically privileged place by personal effort alone. Decades ago, Sennett and Cobb (1972) spoke of the "hidden injuries of class" in the United States. The "hidden injury" is the sense of personal failure when one does not "make it" in the context of an ideology that *anyone* can make it with enough talent and effort. Anyone, that is, except the lazy and personally deficient. Communities, races, and ethnic groups can be tarred with this brush, as well as individuals. The Algerian psychiatrist Frantz Fanon (1963) back in the 1960s explicated how the value systems that rationalized colonial domination and denigrating colonized people created an internalized sense of deficiency and badness.

Psychoanalytically based norms and values only reinforce this structure of privilege and denigration. Community-based mental health programs that rest on this structure of disavowal, projection, and introjection unwittingly reinforce a major source of what is then considered "psychopathology." Well-intended efforts at community mental health need to start with consciousness raising about one's own socialized-in denigrating stereotypes about people who live in economic poverty in our cities and countrysides. A good starting point is an effort to realize that there are advantages to life in the inner city, strengths that are built there; that there are disadvantages, as well, to life in the more economically privileged precincts of the suburbs and cities. The goal of this consciousness-raising effort is not meant to reverse the polarity of value, but rather to complicate it.

When using the word "privilege," as in "white privilege," one rarely finds the type of privilege specified. Nor is the potential disadvantage to any given form of privilege identified and acknowledged. For example, "white privilege" generally refers to economic and political privilege. There are, however, other forms of privilege: the privilege of access to community support, or spiritual privilege. Life among the economically and politically privileged has its elements of disadvantage, as well, a certain treadmill-like pressure to keep up with the Joneses in various ways (Altman, 2010). The fact that privilege is thus invoked without specifying the type of privilege referred to illustrates the degree to which money and power are taken for granted as values in the United States and in many other societies. It is as if there is no privilege to speak of beyond money and political power.

If one is to transcend the mainstream privileging of money and power in the United States and elsewhere, there is no better guide than James Baldwin (1993). As noted above, Baldwin suggests that money and power provide an illusory sense of security in the face of inevitable and ubiquitous human vulnerability to sickness and death. He links the privileges of being white to economic and political power, pointing out the ultimately futile effort to deny the facts of life and death. The tenuous nature of the sense of security attained through money and power is revealed both by the desperate nature of the search for more and more of the same, and by the need for an out-group, in the context of Baldwin's analysis, black people, who are vulnerable and "underprivileged." On a value system that one might call spiritual, or even simply realistic, Baldwin's analysis turns the mainstream United States system of values on its head. Affluent white people in the United States have the "privilege" of trying ever more desperately to assure themselves that they are not black or poor (i.e., vulnerable and mortal). Only the number one top best school or job or income will do, and then not even. Baldwin suggests that humane values flow from the intimate connection with vulnerability, a sense of fellowship with other suffering humans. Judging people by their material possessions or level of income tends to have a dehumanizing effect. Leblanc's (2003) *Random Family*, a study of a family and community in the South Bronx, documents the sharing of money among families on public assistance as they try to make ends meet until the day of the month when the checks arrive. Describing the kinds of situations that tend to come up in such communities, Leblanc wrote:

> Coco's Thorpe House caseworker, Sister Christina, worried about Coco's generosity. When you were poor, you had to have luck and do nearly everything absolutely right. In a life as vulnerable to outside forces as Coco's and her two little girls', the consequences of even the most mundane act of kindness could be severe. The $10 loan to a neighbor might mean no bus fare, which might mean a missed appointment, which might mean a two-week loss

of WIC (a food program for families with young children). Hungry children increased the tension of a stressed household. If the resolution was going to a loan shark, the $10 cost $40 or $50, effectively pushing Coco back a month. But to Coco, nothing was more important than family, and family included Cesar and Lourdes and friends, both new and old. Coco gave Foxy some of her food stamps, because Foxy was feeding seven people on her youngest son's SSI and paying all the bills.

Sister Christina wanted to tell Coco *Get away from your family.* But she couldn't . . . The word that came to Sister Christina's mind whenever she thought of Coco was *enmeshed.* Coco would have said she had heart.

(p. 148)

In a similar vein about mutual responsibility in poor neighborhoods, in this case, the Lafitte Housing Project in New Orleans, Nelson (2005) wrote, describing local store owners:

Most the [sic] store owners were there since their children were babies and know 90% of the neighbors in the community. Its [sic] amazing how people can form a bond from meeting up in these places. We buy and talk because store owners want to know if you're fine and how's the family doing. People can't possibly understand the closeness of public housing until they've lived there.

(p. 35)

And, again:

I always find good neighbors. People who look out for each other's kids or if someone is sick, they'll chip in. These kinds of people exist and in the housing developments they exist. People pull together because most everyone knows just about everyone else's situation. You'd be surprised.

(p. 24)

And:

I live in what can be considered a community; they call it the ghetto. To be honest, for a long time it never felt like a community to me because in a community people help one another by doing anything they can to help a neighbor feel comfortable. But I was wrong and I apologize. Although it took me some time to realize it, now I see.

(p.33)

According to philanthropy.com (http://philanthropy.com/article/Interactive-How-America-Gives/133709/#), the percentage of discretionary income given to charity in the United States falls with income level. Those with the lowest levels of discretionary income ($50,000–$99,000) give 6% to charity, while those with the highest levels (above $200,000) donate 4.2%. The physical structure of life in the United States suburbs, with detached homes ideally with considerable distance from the nearest neighbor, not to mention distance from the poor, reflects the psychological structure of dehumanization. This dehumanization is reflected not only in distance from those to whom suffering is assigned, but also distance from one's own suffering self.

I do not mean to idealize the lives of the marginalized and the poor. Vulnerability does not necessarily breed resilience or humane values. To the contrary, material deprivation can breed self-centeredness and greed as surely as life on Wall Street. Nor does affluence necessarily breed dehumanization. I do mean to complicate the taken-for-granted value system that puts economic and political privilege at the top of the list, with consequences for how people are judged and come to judge themselves. Contrasting value systems, such as that proposed by Baldwin (1993), alert us to alternatives.

The prevailing value system in the mainstream culture of the United States and Europe underlies the ego functions that are privileged in many precincts of psychoanalysis, influencing the value systems organizing some community-based interventions as discussed above. Such interventions, then, need to begin with an analysis of, and reflection upon, the value systems that animate them. Ideally, this occurs in a dialogue with people from the various communities involved. Awareness of racial, social class, and cultural factors is inseparable from this reflection on values. As we have seen, these social factors operate via the value systems that, in combination with linearly organized developmental theories, produce the oppressive hierarchies that distort what otherwise are simply differences between people and peoples.

## The Analytic *Abuela*

One morning, I was reading the *Neighborhood Story Project* volume called *The Combination* (Nelson, 2005) referred to above, in which the community consciousness of the Lafitte Housing Project in New Orleans was discussed. I read sections such as the following, quoted from a neighbor and community resident named Wanda Dubousse:

> Everybody's child was everybody's child. Ashley [the author of this volume, whose mother was addicted to crack cocaine and died when Ashley was a child] was my child. I raised her from a baby. I used to rub her mommy's stomach when she was carrying her. And all the rest of 'em. [Ashley had seven siblings].
>
> (p. 112)

Later that morning, a supervisee arrived to discuss a patient who seemed to be repeatedly enacting an unsatisfying and dysfunctional pattern of relationships in which she would feel bored and dissatisfied with people who were present in her life, such as her husband, in favor of transiently present, but mostly absent figures, men who would come and go from her life, but who were very exciting to her. This woman's mother travelled a great deal for work, turning her care over to her father, from whom her mother had separated and who lived in another country. My supervisee and I were discussing how the men to whom her patient was most attracted were absent, like her mother, although her father was hardly more emotionally available to her when she had lived with him. My supervisee was feeling unsure how to help her patient, and I understood how difficult it is when a problematic emotional attachment is so strong to someone outside the analytic dyad. One feels a lack of therapeutic leverage.

I asked my supervisee what she thought she meant to this patient, who attended her sessions very regularly and on time despite the therapist's sense that she had little to offer her besides her availability. I said to her, "You are an anchor in the midst of chaos." Then I realized that my supervisee's position was like that of Wanda Dubouse. She was the person who was stable in the midst of chaos. The strongest, emotional, and painful attachment was to the absent mother, but it made all the difference in the world that there was someone who was unexciting, but there. My supervisee then recalled how important her grandmothers were to her; we, laughingly, referred to the transference as an *abuela* transference. (The patient was from a Latin American country; "abuela" means grandmother in Spanish.) Noting my bias in favor of transferences to the emotionally charged, "bad object" figures who are usually parents, and devaluing transferences to more stable but unexciting figures such as grandmothers, it dawned on me that this bias was one that derived from privileging the nuclear family in psychoanalytic theory. The real action is associated with the mother and father, the Oedipal parents, not with grandparents, neighbors, siblings, and others in the extended family, or in the community, who might be extremely significant in a more prosaic fashion. Here, I thought, was another example of the bias in psychoanalytic theory toward the nuclear family of Oedipally derived culture.

## Therapists in Goal-Oriented Communities: Schools, Hospitals, and Community-Based Agencies

### School-Based Therapists

School psychology is one form community-based clinical work has taken in the post-World War II years. Sarason, Levine, Goldenberg, Cherlin, and Bennett (1966), outlining the history of the field of psychology, pointed out the crucial role of the Veterans Administration in the early development of psychology as a discipline in the United States. Since the focus was heavily on the treatment of traumatized veterans in hospital settings, the discipline developed an office-based medical model in the United States, focusing heavily on adult men. As a result, community-based work, especially with children and adolescents, fell by the wayside within psychology. Social workers, by contrast, had always done community-based work, focusing on children and families (Sheppard, 2001).

Sarason and his colleagues at Yale sought to fill the gap with a "Psycho-Educational Clinic" in the Department of Psychology. Thus began a long tradition in school psychology, the further development of which is beyond the scope of my expertise and experience. However, I would like to note some aspects of Sarason et al.'s (1966) approach that makes it community based, beyond simply psychotherapy in an office in a school.

Sarason et al. (1966) did not rule out psychotherapy or diagnostic procedures in their in-school work, but they emphasized consultation to the school and its staff. They looked at the school as a system, including their own role as school psychologists. They paid particular attention to the school as having a culture of its own, with centrality given to power relationships. A major aspect of the school psychologist's role, from this point of view, includes the role of consultant (Alpert, 1995; Jacobs, 2012). In Sarason et al.'s (1966) words:

> we had to be part of, and intimately know, the setting in which our services would be rendered. We wished to avoid the consultant role which does not provide the opportunity to observe first-hand the context in which the problem manifests itself. For any problem presented to us it was crucial that we be able to observe the social context in which the problem was perceived, because it was this context that would be the object of change.
>
> (p. 43)

Getting to know the context entailed understanding the experience of teachers, principals and other administrators, students, and parents, both in terms of their generic role in the larger system and the particularity of each individual's experience within his role. For example, Sarason's group emphasized that "Teaching is a Lonely Profession" (1966, p. 74). They wrote: "it is rare that a teacher has the opportunity to discuss her problems or her successes in teaching with anyone else. There is certainly no formal structure for the discussion of the day-to-day concerns of the classroom" (1966, p. 74). Whether this statement is true or not for any given teacher or in any given school, the point is that Sarason et al. (1966) are interested in the experience of the school personnel as it affects their perception of the children about whom they might have concerns, and their perception of the consultant psychologist. Looking at the multidimensional interactions among the people in school-related roles yields a systemic overview within which the consultant is, in Harry Stack Sullivan's words, a participant-observer (Sarason et al., 1966, p. 44). Sarason et al., discussing their work in New Haven, emphasized the salience of the inner-city context for the school's functioning, including their own roles as participant observers. The attention to the school, or school-community, as a system is what makes this approach to school psychology community-based, not just the physical location of the work. This work is community based in a double sense: it is work with a community within the community. The systemic focus operates at all levels, from the microcommunity of a classroom to the macrolevel of the society within which the surrounding neighborhood is contextualized. The systemic focus is also self-reflexive: the psychologist, as a participant-observer, is both part of the community being observed, and the observer, or one of the observers. The community has, as one of its properties, a self-observing function. That is, in fact, what makes a community a human community. Self-observation is cultivated at all levels, from the therapy room to the classroom to the administrative offices at various levels. Psychoanalytic community-based work is oriented toward identifying and opening up one's own, the system's own, blind spots (i.e., the unconscious as it is manifest on individual and group levels).

Music and Hall (2008) took a systemic approach to school-based therapeutic work, beginning with his belief that the child psychotherapist's work in schools consists in "challenging, where appropriate, a discourse about who has a problem, where a problem is located, and how to solve it" (p. 45). Like Sarason, Music believes that the child psychotherapist must "take our clinical skills out . . . into the very fabric of school life" (p. 47). Work with teachers and others in the classroom often focuses on the management of their emotional reactions to their students: "the child psychotherapist can help teachers and management to not only process their own powerful reactions to what they often initially see as 'misbehaviour' but also help them find some sympathy for a child who had hitherto aroused only distaste or anger" (p. 47). Music, in fact, sees some dangers in accepting referrals of children as patients, in that the tendency of adults to project their own anxiety and defensive reactions into children may be reinforced, making children the scapegoats for larger problems in the adults and in the system itself. He writes, "one danger of accepting the referral of individual pupils is that they tend to bear all manner of projections from the system" (p. 50). To reduce this danger, and to keep the therapeutic focus on others in the system and on the system itself, Music advocates not only the work with teachers and other staff mentioned just above, but also with parents, including when the identified patient is an adolescent. Music hopes to disrupt a "culture of blaming" (p. 60) in schools. Yet, perhaps, an even more systemic focus, with an alertness to unconscious enactments, would alert us to focus on how the child psychotherapist may, unwittingly, be sucked into and perpetuate the culture of blaming. For example, it may be difficult, when one thinks that a child is unfairly being blamed, to shift the blame onto the adults. In discussing the case of a girl he calls Courtney, Music writes:

> here was a girl who could be contained, and who responded when the baby feelings in her were looked after. Yet the senior management of the school seemed to experience all Courtney's behavior as an attack of some kind, responding quickly and punitively. She seemed to have become the new receptacle for the negative feelings of the institution as a whole. Our feeling that she was a very worried little girl seemed completely at odds with the formidable presence that rampaged through the collective mind of the staff

room. There was a renewed sense that her exclusion would provide some kind of relief, a fantasy that if only Courtney were got rid of then the school could return to good working order.

(p. 55)

One senses in this passage a view of Courtney as innocent, a "worried little girl" with "baby feelings" while the staff have a "formidable" presence with feelings that "rampaged." Music, properly in my view, called a "Network Meeting" seeking to break through the "cycle of blaming" of Courtney. Yet, a sense that the consultant child therapist is a participant as well as an observer, who could get drawn into blaming someone else for blaming Courtney, could alert the therapist to an unproductive and unconscious enactment. Following the lead of Sprince (2000, 2002), whose work is discussed below, the focus might shift to how the blaming of Courtney, along with the blaming of those who blame Courtney, might reflect a dynamic with roots in early experience, perhaps, and one that Courtney does her own part to perpetuate.

Shepard (2002), discussing articles about school-based mental health interventions by Farley and Manning (2002), Kushce (2002), and Sklarew et al. (2002), pointed out the assumption embedded in these articles that teachers were deficient in emotional literacy. With reference to Kushce's (2002) paper, Shepard (2002) writes "early in the paper [p. 4] she [Kushce] says that teachers do not know how to teach emotional literacy and must be 'trained' to teach it despite the fact that the . . . lessons are scripted" (p. 332). Shepard, a teacher herself, points out that these particular analysts were prone to negative assumptions about teachers that might well interfere with the collaboration they were trying to develop with them. It seems significant that the discussant of the clinical articles (Silverman, 2002) did not address, nor even mention, Shepard's critique. We should not be surprised at the insensitivity and feeling of superiority in relation to teachers; any of us, from any discipline, are prone to insensitivity and prejudice of various sorts. However, we should ask of ourselves that we be open to critique and learning from others, even those whose training is different from our own. Analysts need to learn that they are not immune from the culture of blaming in schools, nor from the human tendency to find someone with whom to feel better, especially when dealing with differences among people.

Maltby (2008) looked specifically at the impact of grief and loss on the life of a school. Often starting with the identification of a problem with a child, Maltby frequently ended up focusing on the impact of a loss in the personal life of a teacher, or the impact of the impending closure of a school, or the loss of colleagues when staff was moved around.

Malberg (2008) described a school-based intervention, run by the Anna Freud Centre in London. The intervention included a supervision of teachers and other staff, and a group for parents aimed to encourage mentalization. Malberg speaks of

adapting and translating our psychoanalytic language in order to develop a common framework between the different systems influencing the life of the young person. It was our refusal to be excluded from the school and family systems and their politics that helped us to reflect on and understand the behavior of some of these young people as a developmental adaptation to a failure of their environment to understand their emotional needs.

(p. 102)

I believe this passage privileges the psychoanalytic perspective and its language in a way that may contribute to psychoanalysts not only being excluded, but excluding themselves from the life of the community. What about learning to speak the languages of the various communities in which one is working, in addition to "adapting and translating" one's own language? In a related vein, it may not help psychoanalysts connect with community people if the starting point is that the problems of their children are a developmental adaptation to their failures. There may, indeed, be some truth to the idea that parents and others in the environment have failed their children (all parents fail their children in many ways) but not all parents, or teachers, or administrators, would be willing to accept that as the starting point of an intervention. Such an assumption may be one way in which analysts exclude themselves from the life of a community.

It is not always, perhaps never, possible for a systemic focus to encompass all levels of a system. Microlevels extend down to the subatomic level, and macrolevels to the universe. Within the human realm of meaning making, however, I suggest that effective intervention requires mindfulness about as many levels of a community as possible. Let us take a private practice office, and then a school, as examples.

The private practice office may seem like a world unto itself; indeed, classical psychoanalysts so regard it when they claim that the only truly psychoanalytic unit of observation is the individual patient's mind seen objectively and in isolation so far as is possible. When the impact of the external world is excluded in this way, the consequence can be that aspects of the patient's experience, even within the private office itself, are overlooked or excluded. For example, the way social class is constructed in the surrounding culture can influence the way the patient perceives self and other around issues like money, the fee requested and paid, the demeanor and attire of the analyst and the patient, the décor of the office, and so on. When the analyst states her fee or opens her door to an office with a certain décor, she locates herself in a social class hierarchy that positions her in relation to the patient's social position. Insofar as social status influences the self-esteem of both analyst and patient, there can be a significant impact on the patient's sense of self that will be expressed in his transference feelings and associations. Regarding these as properties of the patient's mind in isolation would lead to a very different view of the patient than would regarding these as a function of the way analyst and patient have positioned themselves in relation to a social class hierarchy existing in the culture of the world outside the office doors. A patient's feelings of inferiority or superiority in relation to his therapist or analyst may indeed reflect aspects of the patient's mental functioning aside from the social class status of each person as defined in the world outside. The advantage of looking at the private office as contextualized within a larger system is that one has the flexibility of looking at the individual mind, the person's feelings and perceptions, as *both* the qualities of an individual *and* as reflecting a process of socialization and internalization of images of self and others extant in the culture.

Likewise, schools exist within a larger socioeconomic and political context. Under the "No Child Left Behind" regime, for example, a school's, or a principal's, or a teacher's success or failure was purely a function of the adequacy of the individual school or person. Indeed, there may be some justification to such a view. However, taking a wider perspective, one might add questions such as the following: how is adequacy measured or assessed? How do standardized tests as a measure of school performance fit in with a "bottom line" culture? How does it matter that a school is located in a poverty-stricken or affluent community? Does the school in question have more than its share of children who are deprived of educational stimulation at home because of the effects of poverty and discrimination? Is it located in a community where the schools are well funded, or not? Do parents in the community have the option of sending their children to local, religiously sponsored schools, specialized public schools, or charter schools? If so, are the more academically high-functioning children drawn away to these other schools? Here again, taking the larger systemic perspective allows us to look at the qualities of the individual schools as well as the way these qualities are a function of a larger system.

## A Partnership Between a Nonprofit Health Center and a Public School

At a high school in the Bronx, there is an onsite health center jointly run with a health center which is a nonprofit organization in New York funded by city, state, and federal grants and by private and corporate donations, as well as Medicaid reimbursements. This is an economically stressed area of New York City, and is in an alternative high school serving many children with special needs. The grant that funds the partnership pays for a physicians' assistant onsite so students with medical problems can be diagnosed and treated in school. There is also funding for one social worker who provides mental health services. She does crisis intervention and runs therapy groups in the school. Her referrals come from the physicians' assistant, as well as from the guidance counselor and teachers. Notably, students often bring friends to the groups. The social worker reports that supervision is entirely administrative, concerned with documentation of services provided and maximizing billable visits. Although there is no particular requirement for billable visits per week, it is expected that the maximum number of billable visits per week (5.3 visits per day) will take place. There is an end-of-year bonus that is dependent on the number of billable visits for the year. In order to accommodate a large number of students in the school, the psychotherapist is expected to do short-term cognitive-behavioral therapy, short-term trauma interventions, and highly structured ten-week groups. The social worker reports that the atmosphere is "fast, fast,

fast," at least in part to serve the largest possible number of students, as well as to bring in the most Medicaid reimbursements. It seems that in the United States, in New York State and City, the existence of Medicaid reimbursements somewhat tempers the impact of governmental budget cuts. That is, the structure of Medicaid makes it possible to fund a program by seeing a large number of patients, which also means that many students will be served, in however cursory a manner. This funding strategy is successful to the extent that the health center is expanding, including its program in the high school. A licensed practical nurse is being hired to augment the services provided by the physicians' assistant. She is expected to see seventeen patients a day.

### Hospital-Based Therapists

Hospital-based therapists must cope with many of the same challenges as school-based therapists: coordinating with other professionals, trying to find time and space to see their patients, and so on. There is a psychoanalytic literature on working in hospitals in a flexible, systemic way (e.g., Gabbard, 1986; Stanton & Schwartz, 1954) aside from the work of Searles (1965) on psychotherapy with hospitalized patients.

Flynn (1998) described a psychoanalytic-systemic approach to inpatient work, in which transference and countertransference, broadly defined, are seen as circulating throughout the therapeutic community. Patients will have various transference reactions to various staff, including nurses and other staff, as well as to their therapist. These staff members will have countertransference reactions, as well. This pervasive circulation of transference and countertransference blurs the boundaries, using Winnicott's (1986) distinction, between "holding" or "management" and "interpretation." The therapist is trained to recognize and interpret transference and to contain countertransference so as to use her own feelings to therapeutic effect. When transference/countertransference are recognized outside the boundaries of the therapist-patient relationship, the therapist's job must be redefined as recognizing and interpreting transference in the relationships between patients and staff whose job might be narrowly defined as "management," such as nurses and orderlies. The therapist's job might also include helping such staff manage, contain, and put in perspective their countertransference reactions. More broadly, such widely circulating feelings and reactions create a transference/countertransference field, with systemic properties, in which the therapist herself is a participant-observer. The emergence of systemic properties means that the system has properties of its own that organize the personal feelings of patients and staff, with nonlinear dynamics (i.e., dynamics that cannot be reduced to simple, contained, cause-effect relationships). The therapist's job includes pointing out the systemic properties within an inpatient unit, for example, in a way that puts personal, transference/countertransference relationships into a perspective that transforms staff into observers as well as participants. Flynn (1998) describes how this task was engaged not only in community meetings involving patients and staff, but also in "strains" meetings (p. 285) "attended by all the clinical staff, [in which] the emotional impact of the work on the staff is examined, including current pressures and strains between staff. In effect, this looks at the counter-transference processes in the staff working with these patients in a therapeutic community setting" (p. 285).

## Mental Health Work in Community-Based Medical Settings

Many people that are mentally ill or psychologically disturbed, from a Western scientific point of view, present themselves at medical clinics with some sort of physical complaint. Presentation of physical symptoms where one might otherwise find emotional problems is especially likely when and where mental health care is not available, or is heavily stigmatized, or is not the culturally syntonic way of experiencing distress. Workers or agencies who want to address what they see as emotional problems in such contexts sometimes either work through, or alongside, medical workers, doctors, nurses, and so on. Arguably, including this approach would reach the most people in any context, including among urban, educated, affluent people in the West. If mental health workers wish to reach people where they are, addressing problems as they are experienced and recognized, the medical clinic or doctor's office, along with the church or temple or traditional healer or shaman, has much to recommend it. In an effort to facilitate mental health interventions by general health workers, Teaching-aids at Low Cost (TALC) has published a series of manuals that guide health workers in identifying people with mental health and emotional problems, and fashioning interventions that are scientifically sound and culturally syntonic in the local area. Vikram Patel (2002) designed and implemented such a program in Goa, India called "Sangath." He has written a manual for general health workers called *Where There Is No Psychiatrist*.

Since so many psychological problems present as physical symptoms, some mental health workers claim not only that people can best be reached in medical contexts, but that mental health interventions are an important way to reduce societal medical costs. In fact, in the United States, state level mental health initiatives focus on integrating mental health, now referred to as "behavioral health," with general or physical health by emphasizing how people with severe behavioral problems are at increased risk for physical problems because of impaired self-care. The focus is on the cost to the health system of diabetes, linked to obesity, and asthma, in addition to overuse of psychiatric emergency rooms and inpatient units. For example, the Rhode Island Psychological Association writes on its website, http://www.ripsych.org/importance-of-mental-health:

**Mental health treatment reduces medical costs.**

Many research studies have shown that when people receive appropriate mental health care, their use of medical services declines. For example, one study of people with anxiety disorders showed that after psychological treatment, the number of medical visits decreased by 90%, laboratory costs decreased by 50%, and overall treatment costs declined by 35%.

Other studies have shown that people with untreated mental health problems visit a medical doctor twice as often as people who receive mental health care.

Excessive anxiety and stress can contribute to medical problems such as heart disease, ulcers, and colitis. Anxiety and stress can also reduce the strength of the immune system, making people more vulnerable to conditions ranging from the common cold to cancer.

Psychological problems can also increase the likelihood that people will make poor behavioral choices that can contribute to medical problems. Smoking, excessive alcohol or drug use, poor eating habits, or reckless behavior can all result in severe physical problems and the need for medical services.

In New York State, the current redesign of Medicaid emphasizes the integration of behavioral health with physical health and "recovery," which means self-help in the wake of a psychiatric breakdown. Integration of behavioral and physical health is accomplished by focusing on self-care among mentally ill people. Thus, objectives of behavioral health interventions must include improved self-care, such as obesity prevention and blood sugar monitoring.[1]

## Sangath: The Work of Vikram Patel and His Collaborators

Sangath is the name of the mental health program in Goa, India in which mental health paraprofessionals are placed in medical clinics. The program has a research component as well as an intervention model that is summarized in a manual (Patel, 2002). The manual relies on a problem-based model of diagnosis, a cognitive-behavioral and medication-based model of treatment, along with some local traditional and culturally syntonic techniques.

Diagnosis: In an effort to speak to the practical concerns of patients and health workers, categories are problem-based (such as the United States' DSM, or Diagnostic and Statistical Manual, and the World Health Organization's ICD, or International Codes of Diagnosis). Unlike the DSM and ICD, however, this approach to diagnosis seeks to recognize varying types of problems that are likely to be encountered in specific medical settings (i.e., it is context based). Problem-based examples include the person who is violent or aggressive, the person who is confused or agitated, the person who is suspicious, has odd beliefs, or is hearing voices, or the person who is thinking of suicide or attempting suicide. Context-based problems include, for workers in obstetrics and gynecology clinics, the mother who becomes disturbed after childbirth; for workers in geriatric clinics, the elderly person with disturbed behavior; or for workers in pediatric clinics, problems of childhood and adolescence. Another grouping of categories comes under "symptoms that are medically unexplained." Another is "habits that cause problems," like alcoholism and drug abuse. Similar to the DSM and the ICD, this diagnostic approach straddles the line between behavioral and medical perspectives. Within the medical perspective, behaviors become symptoms. There is an assumption, deriving from a medical model, that behaviors/symptoms form syndromes that hang together because there is an underlying physiological basis for the symptoms and the way they appear in clusters. A further assumption, or hope, is that once the physiological basis for a syndrome, or a diagnostic category, is discovered, a medical/medication-based treatment will follow. It is recognized within such behavioral/medical models that behavior-based interventions may also be useful. Once syndromes are established, however tentatively and however tenuous the proposed physiological basis, treatments are proposed and evaluated on an evidentiary basis. The gold standard for evidence is the randomized controlled experiment, in which patients with a particular syndrome (a "disease") are assigned randomly to a treatment, while a control group is assigned to no treatment, or to an alternative treatment against which the proposed treatment is being compared as to efficacy. The outcome is a measure of efficacy, usually defined in one way or another as a disappearance or lessening of the behaviors/symptoms defining the syndrome/disease.

There have been efforts to bring a psychoanalytic perspective to the diagnostic process (McWilliams, 2011; Alliance of Psychoanalytic Organizations, 2006) that focus on the history and meaning of symptoms to the patient. The assumption here is that treatment consists, at least in part, in an investigation of history and meaning (i.e., a psychoanalytic treatment). This approach is consistent with that of Freud who was open to lay analysis (Freud, 1926), even though being a medical doctor. His starting point was the symptom and the idea of treatment. His ending point, however, was history and meaning. This is not the approach taken by Patel (2002), nor by most workers in the community-based clinical field.

Intervention: The forms of intervention recommended by Patel (2002), and by most community-based clinicians, is a combination of psycho-education, cognitive-behavioral psychotherapy, and medication. There are also interventions derived from local and traditional spiritual and healing practices in India, including breathing exercises based on meditation to reduce stress, which is now recommended worldwide by Patel and his group. Patel also advises patients to consult local and traditional healers if they believe their symptoms are caused by spirit possession.

"Talking treatments" as Patel (2002) calls psychotherapy, rely on five principles: give reassurance, provide an explanation, give relaxation and breathing exercises, give advice regarding specific symptoms, and teach problem-solving skills.

Giving reassurance, according to Patel (2002), involves first validating the patient's sense that something really is wrong, when no physical basis can be found for his symptoms. Only then is the patient reassured that what is wrong is not dangerous or life threatening. The reassurance given, thus, is not dismissive, but aims to lead the way to a serious consideration of what *is* wrong.

Giving advice regarding specific problems, according to Patel (2002), involves, first, a kind of reassurance: the problems you are having are quite common. For example, to a woman who is depressed postpartum, Patel advises saying something like, "After childbirth, many women feel pain and discomfort. In fact, it is quite common to feel tired and have sleep problems. Some women may also become sad and lose interest in their baby" (2002, p. 37). Under "giving advice," Patel advises soliciting the patient's view as to what is wrong with her, and recommending local and traditional remedies in addition to the scientifically based treatments that he will recommend. He also advises soliciting and listening to the patient's doubts and concerns.

Relaxation and breathing exercises: Patel (2002) gives step-by-step instructions as to how the practitioner can try out such exercises and guide the patient in doing so at home.

Advice for specific symptoms: For example: "panic attacks result from rapid breathing. Breathing exercises are a helpful way of controlling these attacks" (Patel, 2002, p. 40).

Problem solving: Patel advises explaining to the patient how concrete problems can set in motion psychological reactions that make the original problem worse. For example: "(A) A common problem is not having enough money to meet daily needs. (B) This could make someone turn to alcohol. (C) The person becomes even poorer because he spends precious money on alcohol. (D) His work suffers and he loses his job. (E) This makes him sad and desperate and worsens the drinking and financial problems" (Patel, 2002, p. 41). Patel advises a step-by-step approach to problem solving, from explaining the treatment, to defining the problems, to explaining the relationship between the problems and the symptoms, to defining solutions, taking action, and then reviewing the outcome. Patel cautions the practitioner against trying to solve the problems herself. The goal, rather, is to assist the patient in developing his own problem-solving skills. Patel also gives guidance with respect to counseling in a crisis and about rehabilitation for the chronically mentally ill.

One can see that Patel's (2002) step-by-step approach to "talking treatments" is more complex than it might appear when outlined schematically. For example, he advises soliciting the patient's doubts and questions. He advises soliciting feedback as to the effectiveness of his recommended interventions. However, from a psychoanalytic perspective, he does not prepare the practitioner for the difficulty and complexity of interacting with patients in the ways he prescribes.

Psychoanalysis began with unexpected difficulties encountered in the course of trying to address physical symptoms as psychologically based. Freud and later followers categorized these difficulties and complexities as resistance and transference. Ultimately, addressing the obstacles to the medical treatment became the largest part of the treatment itself. Freud's genius was to conceive that the obstacles encountered in the treatment contained the nature of the disease itself. The management of obstacles (i.e., the interpretation of resistance and transference) became the essence of the treatment. Obstacles became, paradoxically, the *sine qua non* of the psychoanalytic therapy. For example, the idea of transference emerged from a situation in which a patient, called Anna O., professed to falling in love with her doctor, Josef Breuer (Breuer, 1955). Breuer, in those pre-psychoanalytic days, was not able to conceive of Anna O.'s love as the reproduction of an earlier frustrated love that was at the core of her neurosis. Breuer, in a panic (perhaps because of his feelings for *her*, later to be thought of as countertransference), referred the patient to Freud and left on an extended vacation with his wife. Not taking the patient's feelings literally, or Breuer as the literal object of those feelings, Freud was able to see the love as the way the patient was bringing into the here and now the disturbed relationship that had set in motion the neurotic process. Freud (1912) recognized that, paradoxically, transference could serve both as resistance to the treatment, insofar as it led to demands on the analyst for reciprocal feelings, and as essential to the treatment, insofar as it brought the pathogenic forces into the analysis in a vivid way. As he observed, "it is impossible to destroy anyone *in absentia* or *in effigie*" (1912, p. 108). Thus, the figures from the past who had set the illness in motion were brought into the present.

Since Freud's day, the concepts of resistance and transference/countertransference have undergone a great deal of expansion, elaboration, and change. Transference is now widely thought of as referring to all the powerful feelings experienced by patients toward the therapist, derived from the present analytic relationship as well as from the past. Transference emerges from the mutual resonance of past relationships and the current analytic relationship. It is also now widely recognized that countertransference, in the sense of powerful feelings experienced by the therapist toward the patient, are inevitable and ubiquitous. In the context of community-based therapy with economically disadvantaged people, feelings about the economic and power differential between patient and therapist are likely, as are such feelings on the part of the patient. Resentment, envy, guilt, greed, and so on are expectable parts of the transference/countertransference matrix (Altman, 2010). Given these expectable aspects of community-based treatments, it seems to me that a manual such as Patel's (2002) would do well to orient the practitioner to the expectable powerful feelings, both positive and negative, and how they are not only obstacles, but in many ways can potentiate the treatment. I advocate adding something like this:

> People who work with mentally ill people and others with emotional problems are subject to emotional stress themselves. Anxiety and depression are contagious. Some patients will also want you to feel some of what they feel in order to believe that you know what they are talking about, and that you care. You will likely feel anxious and depressed yourself as a result of your work. You will worry about your patients. They may make you angry and frustrated. You will also develop a deep caring and other positive feelings toward many of your patients. You should know that all of these feelings are normal; in fact, they are evidence that you have formed the kind of connection to your patients that can form the basis for you to help them.

Some patients inadvertently may make you feel disturbed, anxious, and depressed as a way of communicating to you some of what they feel. Some patients may feel you cannot really help them unless you know something of what they feel. It may help you to keep your feelings in perspective if you know that your feelings are a result of an effort to communicate on the part of the patient.

Others may inadvertently frustrate you or make you angry as a way of recreating situations from childhood or other times in their lives when they were let down by other people. They may try to recreate with you some of the situations in their lives that contributed to their suffering. Again, it may help you keep your feelings in perspective to think that your frustration or anger with your patients is a result of their unconscious efforts to create with you exactly the kind of interaction that they need help with.

You may feel a deep caring for your patients that can, in its own way, be unsettling. You may worry that your feelings for your patients go beyond what is called for in a professional stance. These feelings are likely evidence of your empathy, compassion, and openness to your patients. They are part of caring enough to allow you to help them. If you have further concerns, you should discuss them with your supervisor or a trusted colleague.

The difference in socioeconomic circumstances, and sometimes racial and cultural differences, may also be cause for unsettling feelings on your part and on the part of your patients. You may be more economically privileged than your patients, and less subject to oppression and prejudice than they are. These differences may be cause for resentment and envy on the part of some patients, and guilt and defensiveness on your part. Cultural differences may make your patients afraid that you will not be able to understand them, or that you will judge them based on standards that are alien to them. These feelings, too, are common and normal for the circumstances; you should keep in mind that you are not expected or called on to share all your patients' life situations or to understand perfectly their cultural practices or meanings. In this respect, as in all respects that have to do with understanding your patients, what is important is that you are *trying* to understand their experiences, and that you are open to hearing about it when you get it wrong. It will help patients in many aspects of their lives if they are able to develop a relationship with you in which they can tell you clearly when they feel misunderstood by you. Misunderstandings happen in all relationships, especially close ones. The ability to sort these out is an important part of building satisfying relationships. You can help in this process by fostering an open and nondefensive atmosphere.

When you do have disturbing feelings with your patients, it helps to know that, for the most part, what you are called on to do is to keep exploring the patient's feelings and experience. If you can help the patient become more aware of what he is feeling and how he is affecting other people, you will have done a lot to improve the quality of his life. Since you will know your patients' experiences to a great degree through your own experience of being with them, it is important that you have support from your colleagues and from your supervisor. Mental health work is hard work, and we all need all the support we can get. When you worry you are not helping enough or that you are not skilled enough, or that you have made too many mistakes, keep in mind that we all have those feelings. They go with the territory.

All parts of a manual such as Patel's (2002) will be most effective if they are part of an in-person orientation in which questions and concerns are raised and addressed in detail, but especially those having to do with feelings in the work (i.e., transference and countertransference in the broadest sense). It may seem unrealistic to expect to orient workers to these levels of deep feeling without ongoing, personal, and detailed supervision. On the other hand, workers will be left to deal with the feelings aroused in the work one way or the other; without such an orientation they will be more on their own, alone. It will be worthwhile if the feelings aroused in this work are normalized, and clinicians are invited to discuss particularly troubling emotional situations with their supervisors. Supervisors, of course, should also be oriented as are the workers.

One might object that the best thing, given the intensity of feelings that can be aroused in psychological work, is to leave them alone, not to stir the pot. One may feel that it is better to stay on a more psycho-educational, and less interactive and emotional, level. Here there is a divide between some psychoanalytic approaches and the more cognitive-behavioral ones. Cognitive-behavioral theory assumes that emotion follows cognition. If you change how people think, their emotions will follow. Emotions do not need to be addressed directly. Some psychoanalytic approaches agree in part; ego psychologically oriented psychoanalysts believe that people vary in their ego strength and it takes a certain kind of psychological strength to manage high levels of emotion and anxiety. Ego psychologists tend to believe that the therapist can manage the level of emotion or anxiety to which the patient is exposed in sessions. Other psychoanalysts believe that emotions are there one way or the other; if not addressed directly, they will express themselves in an uncontained way. Some would even claim that emotions and anxiety are more disruptive when not addressed directly, that they are more out of control when existing in a state of dissociation. Ego psychologically oriented analysts, like cognitive behaviorists, see the therapist as, to a considerable degree, responsible for the session and for titrating the level of emotion and anxiety to which the patient is exposed. Others feel that the session is co-constructed, that patient and therapist are jointly responsible for the fate of the session and the therapy. The latter psychoanalysts recognize that the therapist has a professional responsibility that the patient does not, and should not, have. A useful distinction has been made by Aron (1996) who suggests that a distinction should be made between "mutuality" and "symmetry." According to Aron, "mutuality" means that the patient and therapist mutually influence each other at all times. "Asymmetry" means that they have different roles. Mitchell (1997) commented that the therapist is like a designated driver at a party. He is partying, but is responsible in a way that the other partiers are not. The implication of this middle ground is that workers in the mental health field do need to be prepared to experience and manage high levels of emotion and anxiety, meanwhile to carry on their professional work, even to utilize these feelings in the service of the therapy.

Preventive Interventions: Patel's (2002) manual recommends that preventive interventions be undertaken, both primary prevention (prevention before a problem arises) and secondary prevention (intervention with "at risk" groups). Practitioners are thus enabled to have a wider and deeper impact than they might expect from interventions with individuals who may already have developed serious and entrenched problems, or who face systemic environmental problems that are out of their control, such as poverty, prejudice, and oppression. By recommending preventive and systemic interventions, Patel avoids "blaming the victim," a danger inherent in pathologizing individuals who suffer from societal failures. Patel recognizes that the patient and mental health worker do not interact in isolation. He recommends ways in which mental health workers can advocate for change in the governmental and private sector worlds that support or undermine mental health work. He also recognizes that socioeconomic inequality and oppression are factors in mental illness outside the direct control of mental health workers; nonetheless, they are left to pick up the pieces. Implicitly, he seems to suggest that a feeling of helplessness in relation to the social forces that impinge on mental health work can be corrosive of the morale of people who work in the field.

Among the primary preventive approaches recommended by Patel (2002) are systemic interventions such as political advocacy. Patel suggests that workers consider identifying and supporting candidates for public office who are in favor of measures that are favorable to a community's mental health, such as violence reduction. He also recommends the following primary prevention measures, among others: reduction of mental retardation by encouragement of good prenatal care; support groups for women, facilitation of network building for the elderly; programs aimed at building self-esteem in schools through psycho-education; educational measures to discourage alcohol and substance abuse, and to discourage bullying; dropout prevention programs in schools. Among secondary prevention measures, he recommends support groups for people who have suffered mental illnesses and other measures aimed at relapse prevention, early identification and intervention with behavioral and other problems among children, measures aimed at reducing the stigma associated with mental illness, and measures to assure the human rights of the mentally ill. He advocates early identification of marital and other familial relationships in distress, as well as interventions to repair these relationships or to facilitate a separation when indicated. In all these ways, Patel advocates expanding the job descriptions of mental health workers to include out of office work to reach people where they live, to facilitate changes in the environment and in the daily lives of people to support mental health, to advocate for politicians who support programs that would support mental health in the community, and to lobby for mental health-friendly programs among policy makers.

Community-based mental health work, as envisioned by Patel and his associates, goes far beyond taking psychotherapy into the streets.

Many of the preventive and systemic interventions recommended by Patel are possible because of cultural changes taking place around the world. For example, when a democratic political process takes the place of colonial or other authoritarian rule, it becomes possible to consider political advocacy as a mental health intervention. Scientific findings about tobacco and substance use make it possible to consider psycho-educational preventive interventions in these areas. Upward social mobility and outward mobility (as large numbers of people leave rural areas with their traditional cultures for cities) opens up self-definition and self-esteem as mental health issues. When one's role in life is prescribed based on the traditions of centuries, there are few, if any, options as to how to construct a self. An assortment of new problems arises when people have to make choices in the construction of a self. Preventive mental health interventions to support self-esteem then become necessary and conceivable. The opening up of gender roles and gender expectations creates new possibilities and new dilemmas for both men and women around the world. These developments make it more likely, in recent generations, that women's unhappiness will be attributable to the constraints of their gender role, oppressive behavior on the part of husbands and other male relatives, or domestic violence. What might have been diagnosed as hysteria in the time of Freud, for example, would today be seen as a response to gender-based oppression.

Recall the case of Dora cited above. The case of Dora has been critiqued numerous times by modern feminists (e.g., Moi, 1995) who, with the benefit of feminism, can now see more clearly than Freud, or even than Dora herself perhaps, how she was being exploited. From a postwomen's movement perspective, it is quite clear that the hysterical symptoms and the negative transference itself were "speaking" Dora's resistance to being objectified and exploited. In that patriarchal context, men did not, or could not, hear the message. It was instead read as psychopathology. The symptom replaced the protest in a cultural context that made it unlikely that a direct protest would be received as intended. In the contemporary world, symptoms that had once been read as signs of spirit possession, then of hysteria, now are often read as a protest against social oppression based on gender or other discriminated-against social categories.

There are a myriad of community-based clinical programs in which clinicians, professionals, and paraprofessionals are called upon to meet people with serious mental illness and/or in crisis, in their homes or elsewhere in the community. Assertive Community Treatment (ACT) programs (Stein & Santos, 1998), described more fully above (p. 17), have served seriously mentally ill people in their homes or elsewhere in their communities. In New York City, Parachute NYC/Need Adapted Mobile Crisis Teams (http://www.nyc.gov/html/doh/html/mental/parachute.shtml) provides crisis intervention services from a mobile crisis unit twenty-four hours a day, seven days a week. Workers in all such programs are subject to intense emotional pressures; they would benefit from the sort of support and preparation recommended here in connection with the Sangath program. This is a way that the psychoanalytic focus on transference/countertransference and unconscious functioning can make a crucial contribution in the community, aside from office-based intensive work.

## Consultants in Community Agencies

In Altman (2010), I described the consultative work of Kraemer (2006), Steinberg (2006), and Kraemer and Steinberg (2006) in a neo-natal intensive care unit, and of Sprince (2002) in a therapeutic community for traumatized children. Sprince (2000) and Emmanuel (2002) have also described consultative work with a foster care agency, while Sutton (2002) has recounted work conducted in a pediatric liaison service in a hospital. Sprince and Sutton, based in the United Kingdom, draw on the British object relations tradition of Jaques (1955), Menzies-Lyth (1975), and Bion (1988). Kraemer and Steinberg are United States-based therapists who work with an essentially similar point of view.

Drawing on Bion (1988) in the Kleinian tradition, the British therapists emphasize unthinkable, unprocessable experience, whether as a result of trauma or because of the inadequacy of the person's mental capacity or equipment. When experience is overwhelming or too painful, people resort to a variety of defenses to protect their psychic integrity, including dissociation and projective identification (i.e., seeking to locate the experience in some outside person, in fantasy and/or reality). Abuse and neglect of children leading to foster care, other forms of childhood trauma, and childhood illness, including premature birth, give rise to experiences that are extremely painful, overwhelming, and challenging, if not impossible, to manage. Children and adult patients need defenses to manage overwhelming anxiety: those who seek to help them expose themselves via contagion and projective processes to the anxiety of their charges. Anxiety and the defenses against it operate both consciously and unconsciously in patients and caregivers. Thus, anxiety and the defenses against it circulate, again, via contagion and projective processes throughout organizations that seek to help people who carry with and within them unthinkable experiences. Defenses that entail avoiding and denying anxiety by inducing it in others end up creating conflict within therapeutic organizations that undermines their mission to help their patients. Psychoanalytic consultancy to organizations then is largely devoted to tracking the circulation of anxiety and the defenses against it, then calling these processes to the attention of staff so as to enable them to rethink and renegotiate unproductive situations. Cregeen (2008), citing Obholzer and Roberts (1994), calls this "process consultancy" as opposed to "models of consultancy orientated toward case based advice or expertise, where the disturbance is discussed at one remove, and remains outside the relational processes unfolding in the room" (Cregeen, 2008, p. 174). In this sense, process consultancy is like psychoanalytic treatment more generally: the goal is to raise consciousness about the workings of anxiety and defense with here-and-now vividness. The way enactments ("relational processes") are used to build psychic capacity for anxiety containment is a model for therapeutic processes that can occur at once among the staff and between staff and their charges. In this way, the circulation of anxiety and defense through acting out and splitting is replaced by the circulation of thoughtfulness and reflectivity around experiences of extreme emotion and anxiety.

Jaques (1955) and Menzies-Lyth (1975) described how psychic defenses operate on a group as well as individual level. Menzies-Lyth demonstrated how nurses on a medical inpatient unit, exposed to extreme anxiety around sickness and death, defend themselves against being emotionally overwhelmed in a variety of ways. For example, they divide up work by task instead of by patient, so that one nurse empties all the bedpans while another takes all the blood pressures. No one has total care for any one patient, so no one gets too attached, or too vulnerable to pain when and if the patient dies. Or responsibility for patient care gets kicked upstairs or downstairs through the nursing or medical hierarchy in an effort to avoid guilt. Relief from anxiety and guilt is obtained at the cost of a degree of dehumanization and distance in patient care. Menzies-Lyth also discussed the social defense system operating in residential institutions for children. Again, she saw the fragmentation of care as serving the avoidance of pain for staff members exposed to the unbearable pain of children who had been abused and neglected. Menzies-Lyth elaborated on the nature of the anxieties stimulated by this type of work: children may split off and project into staff members a very harsh and punitive superego. It may take considerable psychic work for staff members to resist taking on a punitive role in response to provocative children, or projecting such an attitude into one of their numbers, becoming disapproving of that staff member's punitive attitude, or becoming overly indulgent in response. This form of splitting among staff was also noted by Gabbard (1986) in hospital settings.

Beyond the psychic strains on the staff, Menzies-Lyth (1985) considered the functional and dysfunctional aspects of organizations, such as residential treatment units, that address extreme psychic pain. In this way, she opened up for consideration a potential community-based role for the psychoanalytic organizational consultant. She emphasized the importance of the authority structure of the organization, and how this structure may serve the social defense system. For example, authority too centralized at the top, or too diffused, may serve a need to avoid a burdensome and painful sense of responsibility for various staff. She gives an example in which housemothers in a residential treatment facility were deprived of the opportunity to participate in the budgeting for food, along with decisions about what to buy. Authority in these matters lay at an institutional level above the housemothers who actually dispensed the food. This structure conduced to blaming of their superiors and helpless resentment on the part of the housemothers about shortages or poor choices of food for the children. The consultant recommended that the housemothers be given money directly to buy food for their charges, while their superiors in the system became advisors to them. The result was an increased sense of collaboration on the parts of all involved, with the housemothers feeling more of a sense of responsibility for their choices in the face of limited resources and the needs of the children. Menzies-Lyth noted that the housemothers thus grew in stature and authority in their own eyes and in the eyes of the children, becoming positive role models for them as they took responsibility for dealing with scarcity and without helpless complaining and blaming. Menzies-Lyth emphasized appropriate boundaries between staff with different roles, as well as the securing of the boundaries of the unit in which the children lived, ensuring that unauthorized people did not enter the unit, for example. She believed that physical boundaries encouraged a sense of identity among those who lived in a given unit, and that this cohesion formed a model for a sense of self with boundaries on the individual level. She believed that caretaking of children should also reflect boundaries with a designated staff member responsible for each child in accord with their skills and competencies. Menzies-Lyth noted that when there was disorganized caretaking, with multiple caretakers responding to whatever needs seemed most pressing at the moment: "these children—identified with—that model, the model of episodic and discontinuous attention, forming in turn a series of episodic and discontinuous relationships with their world through fleeting superficial attachments and also in episodic discontinuous play activities and later in difficulty sustaining continuous attention at school" (1985, p. 201). Menzies-Lyth's work illustrates how organizational consultants' work can take into account psychoanalytic perspectives to analyze how organizational characteristics can create or reinforce social defense mechanisms. These are then shown to ward off pain for the staff at the cost of ineffective functioning in meeting client needs. She points the way toward consultations directed toward organizational change, increasing the ability of staff to contain and process the psychic pain inherent in their work, thus more effectively addressing the needs of the children.

Sprince (2000) commented on a "cycle of blame" (p. 420) that had developed between the social workers in a foster care agency and foster parents. She wrote:

> Social workers, misled by the (biological) parents' plausible explanations, had taken the children into care for a week or two at a time and then returned them. It was the foster carers who fought to get the scale of abuse recognized, and had eventually succeeded. The foster carers were, consequently, virulent in their criticism of the field workers. The field workers reciprocated by invoking policies: the foster carers were the wrong ethnicity, they refused to take on all the siblings and had 'favourites' preferring the ones who were less violent or less damaged. They got too close to the children: this was surely not good practice, as the children might need to be removed after a year or two, and should not be encouraged to bond.
>
> (p. 421)

Sprince's (2000) goal as consultant was to articulate the dynamic origin of this conflict, or split, between the field social workers and the foster parents, so as to open up the situation to change. She writes:

> I talked with all of them about how the cycle of blame that had been established exactly replicated the behaviour of the parents. We discussed how the

policies that were invoked, however useful as a general rule, got in the way of looking at the particularities of the children and this case. . . . We acknowledged that it was much easier to be drawn into the fight than to stay with terrible emotional pain of the children. We thought that a similar dynamic might have been true for the parents . . . they might have sought emotional refuge from their own emotional pain in the buzz of sex, violence, and drugs. . . . It soon became clear to all the professionals how much the ferocious emotional cruelty of these parents, along with their capacity to intellectualize, had infiltrated the entire network, and attacked a capacity to think in the workers as well as in the children.

(p. 421–422)

Note how Sprince identifies an unbearable or nearly unbearable emotional pain, the defenses against it (blaming someone else for the problems) and how the defenses disable the mission of the organization (i.e., to work together for the welfare of the children). The "therapeutic" strategy is to articulate how the conflict between field social workers and foster parents defensively distracts from taking in the pain of the children by assigning a cause (blame) for the pain that is outside oneself, thus relieving oneself of guilt and helplessness. Sprince does not quite articulate how she gets the social workers and the foster parents to renounce the temptations of defense by blaming each other, beyond mobilizing a previously disabled desire to know the pain of the children by pointing out how all parties were avoiding that experience. Perhaps the consultant's authority and commitment to the welfare of the children allowed all parties to transcend their defensive emotional blaming.

In another article, Sprince (2002) emphasized that the consultant's credibility with workers who are struggling to contain extreme anxiety and emotion depends on the consultant's demonstrated ability to do the same. Workers may induce anxiety, guilt, and pain in the consultant not only for their own defensive purposes, but also a) so that the consultant will know by experience what the workers have to bear, and b) to see if the consultant can bear it. Sprince (2002) writes, with reference to her work in a therapeutic residence:

The school selected the children they would send my way, and I found myself confronted with a series of large teenage boys who threw chairs at me, threatened me with sharp knives and cigarette lighters or tried to strangle or rape me. I was never hurt, but I was frequently terrified. I recognized, pretty quickly, that the teachers and care staff were organizing referrals that would ensure that I would get to have the frightening and overwhelming experiences that they endured. . . . They were setting me a test: if I could survive and still come out able to think about the children's feelings, they would begin to trust my way of working.

(p. 147)

With her mind invaded in this way by the experiences she was trying to help the staff contain, Sprince (2002) learned that she must look to her own experience as a guide to what the children and the staff had to endure. Sprince comments:

> Over several years this young man had filled me with a series of shocking and painful emotions: terror, outrage, murderous anger, panic, despair, and most disturbingly, moments of sexual arousal accompanied by intense shame, disgust, and self-loathing. Anyone who works closely with these children will have similar experiences: through the ordinary human mechanisms of empathy and intuition we find ourselves, at certain moments, feeling their feelings and the feelings of their abusers.
>
> (p. 148)

Having attained this knowledge by acquaintance, Sprince could help the workers identify and think about the extreme emotions circulating through the system, cutting through the defensive processes that previously had set in motion the splits and conflicts that had set the staff against one another, interfering with the mutual support and work orientation necessary to work effectively in this environment.

Emmanuel (2002), consulting in a child welfare agency, emphasized the workers' and foster parents' need for support in order to bear the experiences induced in their work with foster youth. She writes, with regard to psychotherapy with foster youth: "Focusing exclusively on the child without attending to the needs of the carers can leave professionals and foster and adoptive parents feeling neglected and misunderstood, and, without their active co-operation and alliance, any efforts to treat a child are likely to fail or be undermined in some way" (p. 165). Emmanuel notes how rivalries and envy break out when some feel that others' (including the children) are getting more support and nurturance than they. Child therapists, as well as consultants, need to be aware of the way the impact of their intervention ripples through the surrounding system.

Cregeen (2008) and Reeves (1979) describe their respective work as consultants to residential treatment units for adolescents (Cregeen) and children (Reeves). With a nod to Selma Fraiburg et al.'s (1975) concept of "ghosts in the nursery," Cregeen (2008) refers to the ghosts left over from "trans-generational deprivation and abuse" (p. 175) that create "multiple phantoms within the adolescents (that are) carried into the care setting, which seek refuge, attention, and containment" (p. 175). Processes of dissociation and defense give rise to "psychic no-go areas" (p. 175) for both carers and adolescents, creating areas of unreflective acting out. Cregeen, looking at the psychic situation of the workers, refers to

> worker anxieties about their own goodness, competency and capacity to tolerate emotional states (which are) stirred up by work with young people whose lives bear witness not only to familial failures but also to societal ones. . . . The potential for effecting sufficient repair can often be hugely

compromised . . . blame is readily mobilized as adolescents and workers seek to manage their experiences of guilt, helplessness, and fury. For the workers, this is complicated because although they often see themselves in a rescuing role, the transference from the young people includes that of failing parental figures.

(p. 174)

Cregeen sees the consultant's job, in relation to the staff, as follows: "to be able to understand the nature of their anxieties and conflicts, bear the negative transference and retain a sense of hope. By hope, I mean the belief that meaning can be discovered, whatever the circumstances or the suffering" (p. 175). There could hardly be a more clear statement of the credo that animates psychoanalytic work with individuals and groups.

## Note

1  See Office of Mental Health Continuous Quality Improvement Initiative for Health Promotion and Care Coordination: 2013 Project Activities and Expectations, retrieved from http://www.omh.ny.gov/omhweb/psyckes_medicaid/webinar/cqi_initiative.pdf

# Chapter 7

# Globalization and Mental Health

## Neo-Colonialism, or Neo-Liberalism, and Mental Health

Since the fall of the European colonial empires in Asia, Africa, and Latin America, a new regime has emerged that is called, variously and depending on one's attitude toward it, globalization, global capitalism, neo-liberalism, and neo-colonialism. In this section, I will review the characteristics of this new world order, some political attitudes toward the system, some of its effects and manifestations—including its effect on mental health systems, public and private—around the world.

### Some Background

"Globalization" refers to both an economic system and an associated constellation of cultural shifts. On the economic side, global capitalism is made up of multinational corporations and the capital they control moving freely across national borders for purposes of investment and the buying and selling of natural resources and commodities. Alongside the autonomous nation-state with its local economy regulated by national and provincial governments, there is a transnational economy composed of multinational corporations headquartered in one country and operating in multiple countries. Each nation has the power to regulate and tax the operations of multinational corporations within its borders; nations also try to protect their local economies from negative outside influences by, for example, restricting immigration, imposing tariffs on imports, and influencing interest rates and the value of its currency compared to other currencies. Nation-states also create economic unions, such as the European Union, or the North American free-trade zone, within which tariffs are suspended so that goods can be produced wherever the cost of production is lowest, and can be moved freely (i.e., without tariffs) between nations within the union. Supporters of global capitalism cite the way it may promote innovation and creativity by economic incentive and its economic efficiency as corporations and other businesses seek out the lowest cost labor and raw materials on a global basis, while seeking out markets around the world. Costs of goods, in general, may be lower under this system as the costs of production go down. Critics of global capitalism cite the diminished power of labor to advocate for and negotiate working conditions and wages, as employers are free to move work to another country. Critics also point out that corporations are answerable to their shareholders, who are primarily or solely interested in monetary profit. When corporations are less answerable to governments, especially democratically elected governments, they are less likely to be concerned with the public interest. For example, local pollution is less likely to be of concern to a multinational corporation than to a locally based company, though the multinational corporation still has an interest in local public relations. Multinational corporations have an interest in global climate change, though this has relatively long-term consequences, and shareholders are most likely to be interested in short-term profits. With a global labor force, corporations are less likely to be interested in hiring people for the long-term; they are interested in being able to hire people here for one project, there for another, according to where they find people with particular skills at a particular wage, or fee. Large multinational corporations are less likely to be concerned about the long-term health of their employees, including their mental health. Hiring people part-time without health and other benefits saves the corporation money and increases shareholder profit. The United States health care plan enacted in the Obama administration was proposed as a response to this situation in which corporations are less motivated to provide for the health of their employees by substituting the government as the guardian of the public interest, or of the welfare of those whom the corporation may not be motivated to protect. Intense opposition to this plan arose from those who believed public as well as private interests are best served by the free operation of the markets, including financial markets, markets for goods, and markets for labor. The theory is that healthy corporations are more likely to create jobs and hire people, while overly taxed and regulated corporations are hindered in their ability to create jobs and to hire people. Critics of the critics respond that corporate profits are more likely to benefit shareholders and go toward raising executive compensation. Critics of the critics of the critics in turn respond that most citizens, at least of some countries, are direct or indirect (through their pension plans) shareholders in multinational corporations. Critics of the critics of the critics of the critics point to the vast number of people worldwide who have no pension plans. Clearly, it makes sense to seek some balance between the benefits of global capitalism and some government regulation to rein in its excesses and its relative indifference to the public interest and the fate of those who are left out from its benefits, or who are injured by the system.

As an example, consider the situation of farmers in Asia. Multinational agribusinesses bioengineer high-yielding seeds, thus increasing food production to feed a huge and growing population in a country like India. It is in the economic interest of the shareholders of such corporations, like United States-based Monsanto, to patent the bioengineered seeds in order to control the production and marketing of their products. These corporations go further, however, advocating for laws to make it illegal for farmers to gather their own seeds from the crops grown from patented seeds. The cost of food production rises as the cost of seeds rises, squeezing farmers to the point of thousands of bankruptcies and farmer suicides in recent years in India. Here is a devastating human cost to pay for global capitalism. Supporters of free market capitalism would point out that the system also feeds many people who would otherwise starve or go hungry, and may also benefit farmers by providing them with global markets for their crops. There are similar issues involved with multinational pharmaceutical companies. Supporters of these companies would point out the major advances in the treatment of diseases all around the world due to research and development of innovative drugs, which are financed and incentivized by global profits from patented drugs. Patents price these drugs out of reach of large numbers of people. In the case of both bio-engineered seeds and drugs, there is a need for government regulation to balance the benefits of the global capitalist system with the needs of those who are injured or left behind.

It should be clear from this discussion so far that the issues involved in global capitalism, its benefits and liabilities, are complex and multifaceted. One-dimensional pro and con positions are likely to oversimplify these issues. Nonetheless, there are times when one is called upon to take a political position: for example, when choosing among candidates for public office who take strong positions for or against free trade zones or government regulation of the financial industry, or when lobbying or advocating among politicians on such issues.

A related point is that advocates of a particular position may dismiss the arguments of the other side as hypocritical and/or manipulative. Protestations by multinational corporations of concern with the public interest, with social justice, or with environmental sustainability, may be dismissed by some as cynical and hypocritical public relations ploys.

## What's in a Word?

There is rhetoric in support of one-dimensional positions that seek to influence people, sometimes at the cost of complex and independent thinking. For example, in writing this section, when I use the term neo-colonialism, I am attempting to influence the reader to regard the phenomenon as continuous with colonialism with all its connotations of exploitation and violence. If I use the term "global capitalism," I may be using a term with positive or neutral connotations for some readers, while for others, I may be evoking the ghost of Karl Marx and his analysis of the exploitation of workers. The term "globalization" is more likely to evoke a positive or neutral connotation with respect to the system, or regime, the latter term evoking an image of totalitarian coercion. When advocates of global capitalism refer to the pre-1991 socialist orientation of the Indian government as the "license raj" (Mazumdar-Shaw, 2013), the rhetoric implies that the government at the time was high-handed to an extent that would befit a king (the Hindi meaning of "raja"). The point here is that such rhetoric seeks to bypass independent thinking based on consideration of various sides of a question. It is true that it is impossible to discuss any issue from a completely unbiased perspective, but the use of overdone rhetoric seems to imply insecurity about whether the reader will come to a reasonable conclusion on the merits of the argument.

Another example is the co-optation of the word "progressive" by people on the left to refer to their policies. The use of the word seems to preempt thought with language (In what direction do we want to progress and why? What are the possible unanticipated consequences of moving in a particular direction?). People on the political right, of course, never refer to their policies as regressive, though they may spin the debate by calling their policies "conservative," without noting what elements of the status quo they wish to preserve and why. Inevitably, advocates of global capitalism have been calling policies that enable free markets "progressive," as well (e.g., Agarwal, 2013, p. 254, writes of "progressive mining policies," referring to less government interference in the mining of gas and oil).

Some terms, like "liberal," have interestingly changed their meaning as the political and economic context has changed. In the mid-to-late-twentieth-century United States, "liberal" was set in contrast to "conservative." Conservatives advocated maintenance (to "conserve") of the status quo. Liberals (from "liberal," deriving from the word for "free" in Latin) meant to advocate change (i.e., to be free enough from tradition or the status quo to change). The Civil Rights movement was a case in which preservation of the status quo was set against freedom to change the system. Today, this word signifying freedom is more likely to refer to a position that favors "free" markets. The shift is acknowledged with the prefix "neo-." Below, I will come to some of the rhetoric that reveals the shifts in values associated with global capitalism.

## History

In the colonial age, multinational corporations, generally based in the United States and, to a lesser extent, in Europe, operated in a patchwork fashion mostly in Latin America. For example, the United States-based United Fruit Corporation controlled much of the production of fruit in Latin America for sale in the United States. The United States-based Anaconda Copper Corporation controlled the production and export of copper in Chile. Asia's economies operated, for the most part, on a socialist system that excluded the entry of such corporations, limiting the development of multinational corporations in Asia. Where multinational corporations operated, producing resources and commodities crucial to the United States economy, the United States government often operated secretly through the Central Intelligence Agency (CIA) to support governments that were friendly to the multinational corporations, and to undermine governments that were unfriendly to the corporations. The CIA established the "School of the Americas" to train Latin American officials in techniques, including the use of torture, in support of the stability of "friendly" (i.e., right-wing) governments. "Friendliness" to the multinationals was and is generally associated with affiliation with a "free market" ideology that opposes government interference in the economy and in the operations of corporations. "Unfriendliness" is generally associated with support for government regulation of business in interest of government-provided social services and a social safety net. A notorious example is Chile, where the socialist government of Salvador Allende in the years from 1970 to 1973 prioritized government regulation of the economy in the interest of the provision of social services, a social safety net, and a relatively equal distribution of income across the population. Because this socialist system operated to restrict the operations of the multinational corporations, the CIA supported its opponents who eventually overthrew Allende, ushering in the dictatorship of Augusto Pinochet who killed and tortured his opponents until he was ousted in an election in 1990. Such violence ostensibly on behalf of an economic system, which was matched by such advocates of socialism as the Soviet Union and Cuba, makes clear that we are talking about regimes of power as well as about theories of how to maximize human welfare. Interest in spreading one's favored political and economic system throughout as much of the world as possible leads some to speak of "neo-colonialism." The fall of the Soviet Union in 1991, combined with the fact that global domination is at the heart of the regime of globalization and free market theory, seems to have entrenched global capitalism except for isolated pockets around the world.

Having presented the issues involved in such stark terms, one must take a step back and acknowledge that, for the most part, advocates of global capitalism make more or less room for state regulation and provision of infrastructure, while advocates of socialism make more or less room for private enterprise. How this balance has played out in different countries is influenced to a great extent by the prior colonial history. In India, for example, the British colonial regime exploited cotton farmers in India to supply cotton to British mills, which would then sell finished products to people back in India at a profit, all of which went to England. One of Gandhi's major initiatives was to encourage Indians to produce their own cotton, called "khadi," that is, to make themselves independent of the British in this respect. It is small wonder that in the postcolonial years, the Indian government highly regulated foreign-based corporations and was resistant to foreign investment. The resistance to foreign investment led to the system in India being referred to, contemptuously, as a "license raj" (as noted above) by advocates of globalization, referring to the control the government had over the granting of licenses to foreign corporations to operate in India. It was not until 1991 that the Indian government began to open up to foreign multinational corporations, a process that is ongoing. The so-called Communist regime in China is now quite open to highly regulated private enterprise and participation in global markets; there is considerable debate about the role of government regulation of markets in the paragon of free markets, the United States. Clearly, however, the move in the last twenty-three years has been strongly away from public regulation of markets and of private enterprise. The deregulation of the financial markets in the United States caused the near meltdown of 2008, as banks and investment houses sold financial instruments that were based on unsustainable mortgages, instruments the investment houses themselves knew were bound to collapse. What is notable is that the fallout from this debacle has been the starving of the public sector and the diminished role of government throughout the world, rather than increased regulation of markets and of the players who fund global capitalist activities. Ironically and tragically for many, it appears the abuses allowed for by free global markets is to be paid for by the public sector, an outcome that could not have been more welcome to those who favor free markets, and less welcome to those who favor an expanded role for the public sector in the support of human welfare. The pendulum, seemingly inexorably, has been swinging to the right (Stiglitz, 2003).

## Globalization and Mental Health

Let us now turn to the cultural meanings of "globalization" in terms of the psychological implications and consequences of global capitalism for mental health and for the systems that serve the mental health of human beings. Turning first to the psychological dimensions of global capitalism, clearly the system privileges competitive and achievement-oriented values. The competitive framework for capitalism is manifest in the use of the word "player" to refer to market participants, as though the whole thing were a sporting match. Economic systems that privilege communitarian and collaborative values on a larger scale are more likely friendly toward a larger role for government in distributing resources through taxation of the well to do, with programs that benefit the less well to do. These delineations are not absolute. Corporations require and value collaborative work within corporate boundaries, while socialistic systems have given rise to a great deal of competition in the realm of political power and control. Corporations donate to nonprofit organizations that benefit the poor, even if the motivation is self-interested, for public relations, for example. As a rule, however, the ideology of capitalism is that monetary incentives are what motivate people to produce and be creative, which in turns benefits everyone as jobs multiply. The underlying theory of human nature is that people are fundamentally materialistic, acquisitive, and self-interested. Socialist systems, ironically, often have the same assumption, giving rise to the idea that government must regulate what people do in the interest of social justice and equity in the material realm. The notion that people may be motivated, primarily or secondarily, to benefit their fellows materially, psychologically, or spiritually, is, at least in the West, consigned to religion. From a religious/spiritual point of view, Baldwin (1993) argued that the competitive, materialistic values of capitalism, which he regarded as culturally European, or white, were based on an illusion. The illusion Baldwin had in mind was that material comfort or security would provide immunity from the common human condition of mortality and vulnerability to aging, illness, and so on. The idea that people commonly seek to deny the fact of death was put forward by Becker (1973) who, following Rank (1936), suggested that much human activity is devoted to achievements and productions that give the illusion of permanence. In Becker's wake, Greenberg, Solomon, and Pyszczynski (1997) put forth "terror management theory," according to which people develop "cultural worldviews" that give meaning to life, which may entail beliefs in life after death, achievements that transcend individual life, and identification with groups that outlive the self. According to terror management theory, people tend to consolidate beliefs and attitudes in synch with their preferred cultural worldview when their awareness of mortality and vulnerability is increased. Hypotheses based on this theory have been confirmed in a number of different situations. This theory produces an explanation for stereotype formation of out-groups and prejudice based on the need to maintain one's cultural worldview against other competing worldviews. Terror management theory, like Baldwin's perspective, sees difficulty in accepting the fact of our common human vulnerability and mortality at the root of a great deal of human behavior, including much destructive behavior. From the point of view of terror management theory, Baldwin's perspective leads to an alternative value system, a cultural worldview, based on the belief that feeling for the suffering of our fellow human beings (i.e., love and a sense of community) gives meaning to life. In an article called *Manic Society* (Altman, 2004), I followed Baldwin and suggested that the promise of immunity from suffering leads people to chase money, material comfort, and security more and more desperately as it becomes clear that whatever material benefits had been attained would not confer immunity to vulnerability, nor give meaning to life. The fact that the more economic privilege people have, the faster they run on the various treadmills, and this gives evidence of the emerging preconscious awareness that no amount of money or power fulfills the implicit promise of capitalism. Thus, the ever-accelerating pursuit of money, the right college, even the right nursery school, reflects a manic defense against awareness of the human condition. Wachtel (1989) made a similar point, writing: "we have lost track of what we really need. Increasing numbers of middle class Americans are feeling pressed and deprived, not because of their economic situation—we remain an extraordinarily affluent society . . . but because we have placed an impossible burden on the economic dimension of our lives" (p. 2). Wachtel (1989) points to the "problem posed by our anxious reliance on the production and accumulation of goods to compensate for the decline in other more traditional sources of security" (p. 79). Curry (2005) pointed out that in the United States, many adolescents seem to have given up caring about their own welfare, turning to a variety of self-destructive behaviors with an attitude that nothing really matters. In his book titled *The Road to Whatever,* Curry (2005) suggests that since everyone is aiming for the top, anything less than the best feels like failure. Most people in a society with this level of competition are going to feel like failures, succumbing to the "whatever" syndrome that Curry identifies. In that sense, the extreme competitive values associated with global capitalism are bad for mental health. A utopian, uncritical commitment to socialism may be damaging for mental health to the extent that those with political power may feel entitled to impose their values on people presumed to be "counter-revolutionaries." The more virtuous people feel, the more they may feel entitled to impose their values on others, often violently.

In other ways as well, a socialist or "welfare state" system can have its own potentially negative set of consequences for mental health. At the extreme, such a system can foster dependence and passivity while discouraging initiative and creativity. As Fromm (1947) pointed out many years ago, economic systems promote personality styles and values that reflect the nature of the system while producing behaviors that are adaptive to that system. There are extremes and caricatures of such "social personalities" that may develop and become pervasive in a given cultural context as well. Global capitalism thus adaptively fosters independence, initiative, ambition, creativity and, less desirably, greed, arrogance, and intolerance of dependence. Socialism adaptively fosters community feeling, cooperation, inter-dependence and, less desirably, passivity and extreme dependence.

Socialization into capitalistic values can lead to unreflective adoption of these values, with blind spots about other possible value systems. For example, Werbner (1998), discussing pilgrimages to Sufi shrines in Pakistan, notes that pilgrims engage in sacrificial activities to produce food for free distribution to those in need in dining facilities called "langars." They take home souvenirs from the shrines in order to retain something of the holiness of the saint. She notes:

> My interpretation of the acts of sacrificial service, and the act of sharing in a sacrificial meal at the lodge, stresses the need to unmask a self-interested discourse in order to reveal the central experience of altruism and humanism which energises Sufism. My argument thus reverses a common sociological tendency to seek material interests beneath the surface of apparent altruism. In Sufism, a discourse of market relations and patronage is used by suppli- cants to 'explain' their relation to the saint, alive or dead. Given an occidental tendency to seek self-interested motives behind apparently altruistic facades, this Sufi allegory of interested exchange may easily be accepted at face value, as a 'true' explanation of supplicants' motives.
>
> (p. 97)

Werbner (1998) points out here how her readers with capitalistic values may unreflectively assume that there is a self-interested motive that is more fundamen- tal than the spiritually derived values promulgated in Sufism. She writes:

> If sacrifice in Islam hinges on the existence of inequalities, of a category will- ing to define themselves as 'poor,' it nevertheless also encompasses notions of moral responsibility within a moral community. The langar objectifies the moral community embodied by the saint himself as a figure of infinite generos- ity. This underlines the fact that in Islam voluntary labour, sacrifice, donations, offering and charity merge. All these acts are vehicles mediating the relationship between person and God. In all, moral space is extended, objectified and per- sonified, while the identification between person and community is revitalised.
>
> (p. 112)

## Mental Health Systems in the Age of Global Capitalism: Commodification and Objectification of Human Beings

Commodification refers to the process by which things become items to be bought and sold. The value of a commodity is usually measured in terms of money (i.e., a symbol and metric for economic value). Commodities can be bought and sold in a barter system as well. Many things, such as food and clothing, have been bought and sold for centuries, though in the context of subsistence farming and home-spun clothing, such items can remain outside the system of commodification as it exists within capitalism. In recent years, with the supremacy of global capitalism, services, information, knowledge, and human capacities have also become com-modities in the sense that they have been thought of in terms of economic value. The process of commodification has recently been referred to as "monetization." For example, if someone has a good idea for a service, the question might come up as to whether and how it can be "monetized." Human beings themselves become commodities as slaves in which they are bought and sold, or in less extreme form, when they are bought and sold as athletes. Fromm (1947) described the way peo-ple can develop a "marketing personality" under capitalism. He was referring to the process of commodification of human beings and their capacities so that people market themselves, or their selves, as a way of being. Commodification can become so taken for granted that people may forget that value can be defined in ways other than economically. Value, including personal value, can become synonymous with economic value. People objectify other people and themselves; self-esteem can be profoundly affected by the degree to which one's skills, capaci-ties, and interests can be monetized. In relatively unregulated capitalism, some people can accumulate so much money, with their wealth widely publicized in the mass media as they become celebrities, that the self-esteem of many people can become tied to the position where they stand in relation to fantastic norms. On a less grand scale, television and movies can make a certain level of material luxury seem standard, so that the great majority of people's self-esteem can become tied competitively to the level of material possessions acquired by fictional characters. With the rise of mass media, the impact of the way lives and people are portrayed, especially on television, has mushroomed. Advertising builds on peoples' fan-tasies of the young, beautiful, rich, and famous to sell goods and services with the implicit promise that one can thereby become one of "them" with the swipe of a credit card. The pervasive cultivation of such illusions has grown geometri-cally in the last few decades as many people, isolated in their suburban homes, spend more and more time watching television. At the same time, income inequal-ity has increased dramatically so that more and more people, left off the gravy train, are spending increasing amounts of time watching and identifying with the materially privileged. This phenomenon is most pronounced in the United States, but with the spread of global capitalism, it is rapidly spreading throughout the rest of the world. Correspondingly, other, nonmaterial, forms of value become de-emphasized. In the contemporary United States, and increasingly around the world, people who work with money, buying and selling shares of companies, trading currencies, and so on, are compensated at a level many times that of people who care for or educate children, or adults for that matter. Traditionally female occupations are compensated poorly compared to traditionally male occupations. In this way, the value system underlying gender bias, and other forms of bias, is manifest and perpetuated.

One genre of television show seems to aim at naturalizing competitive values and promoting subordination to the domination of the super-rich. On the *Celebrity Apprentice*, celebrities are assigned tasks in groups by Donald Trump. At the end of each episode, one celebrity is fired. Trump, matter of factly and unfeelingly, says to the celebrity, "you're fired." The celebrity, an otherwise admirably successful artist or performer, submissively walks away and disappears. People are thus socialized to being fired. They learn that it's a tough world out there. On *The Bachelor* and *The Bachelorette*, people compete to be chosen by an attractive young person of the other gender to get married. (S)he tries out one, then another, looking for the man or woman with whom (s)he will fall in love. At the end of each episode, the bachelor or bachelorette chooses who will stay, and who will go. Toward the end, one very hopeful contestant is deselected, being driven away into oblivion, dejected and/or angry, in a chauffeured limousine. These shows, as well as others such as *The Millionaire Matchmaker*, put forth the idea that the love of one's life can be found by a man or woman who carries certain possessions or personal qualities. For men, in general and unsurprisingly, money is the *sine qua non*. For women, equally unsurprisingly, the necessary but not sufficient quality is attractiveness. It doesn't hurt if the man is attractive as well. All concerned must want to "settle down," get married and have children, usually after a life of playing the field or unsuccessful attempts at mating. Beyond that, the one who is looking for love in each episode has a list of desired qualities for the sought-after love of his life. She must be intelligent, fun, dynamic, whatever. Reflecting the online dating culture of the time, the assumption seems to be that the right combination of personal and demographic characteristics makes for love and/or the right mate. Ironically, the setup seems reminiscent of the old-school arranged marriage, in which mates are chosen based on being from the right family. Love, hopefully, will follow. In short, on these shows, people are objects, commodities, to be selected, fired, married, or sent away by the super-rich, super beautiful people who are masters of the system.

## Commodification of Psychotherapy

Psychotherapy, like any service, has become a commodity in the context of capitalism. Consider some of the consequences: psychotherapy is branded and marketed like any commodity, offered to people as a service that can, quickly and magically, make one happy. Thus, there is a multiplicity of psychotherapies with brand names (I recently saw a plaque in Manhattan announcing a practice in "cognitive health") marketing themselves as "evidence based" (short-term quantified outcome studies) making people more functional and, implicitly, happier. Longer-term psychotherapy, psychoanalysis in particular, has a branding problem. Freud's (Breuer and Freud, 1893–1895) promise of "ordinary human misery" replacing "neurotic suffering" (p. 305) is an especially difficult slogan to sell to people.

A recent email message sent at Christmas time to the staff of a public mental health clinic shows the impact of the commodification of psychotherapy in the public sector in a particularly stark form. The director, announcing the availability of Christmas gifts for economically impoverished patients, urged the staff to give them out. The clinic is largely funded by Medicaid; attracting patients to the clinic one way or another is key to bringing in revenue. The message asked the staff to remember the debt of gratitude that they owe to their patients for attending sessions, thus funding staff jobs. The staff should therefore be happy to return the favor to their patients with material gifts. If any staff had problems with gift-giving in her "practice" (seemingly an acknowledgment of the remnants of the psychoanalytic ethos of a bygone era), she should discuss her misgivings with the director.

This message acknowledges that patients do take care of their therapists in an economic sense; this is an aspect of the mutuality of the psychotherapeutic interaction that is more evident in private practice. What is striking is that the return gift of psychotherapeutic help is absent from the calculation. Such intangible help does not show up on the radar screen of a culture organized around material, and magical, exchange. There seems to be a special denigration of the economically disadvantaged population's capacity to respond to the offer of specifically psychotherapeutic help.

Suffering obviously remains on reality television and everywhere else. In fact, the pursuit of the illusion of happiness through material privilege seems to contain its own undoing, its own form of generation of further suffering. Obviously, given the skyrocketing levels of inequality, there is a huge, and increasing, amount of economically based suffering out there. Other forms of suffering continue as always. The commonplace suffering these days generated by people losing their homes, their jobs, their health, and so on rarely finds a place in the popular media, although it is reported and explored in serious news programs, newspapers, and magazines. Such ongoing suffering and lack of privilege is reflected on television shows such as *Teen Mother* and *Dr. Phil* in the form of highly sensational life meltdowns. These meltdowns are certainly more common and likely under the conditions of stress generated by economic hardship and failures of the safety nets provided by government, families, and community. In the popular media, however, life crises and self-destructive behavior are presented as dramatic individual and family pathology and dysfunction. These seem to attract viewers by presenting suffering as entertainment, appealing to a certain schadenfreude (pleasure in the suffering of others) and generating a sense of moral superiority among viewers who can look down on the "poor life choices" made by the shows' stars. As best-selling entertainment, these shows commodify suffering, appealing to viewers/consumers and advertisers, by resort to histrionic and manic devices that can serve to captivate and distract large numbers of people.

## Linear Currents, Nonlinear Dynamics

We are living in the midst of vast and rapid social changes associated with the supremacy of global capitalism and technology. Technology has linked us and divided us from ourselves, dehumanized and objectified us; it has enabled capitalism to become global, enabled new opportunities for creativity and communication, for sharing of experience and for being distracted from painful experience. Most of all, the pace and scope of change has disoriented us and made us struggle to articulate what is happening and who we are becoming. As can be seen in my own reflections, there seems to be no way to understand where we are headed except in terms derived from the past. With our feet planted in the familiar, we try to divine the significance of the hints of the future coming down the pike. If there is one thing that *does* define this new age, perhaps it is that the past offers less and less reliable guidance as to how to prepare to orient ourselves to the future.

In this way, the evolution of psychological theory and psychotherapy can be seen to reflect social and cultural evolution. In classical psychoanalytic theory, the present and future were largely determined by the past. Personality and psychological dynamics were regarded as largely set by middle childhood, age six or so, and the "resolution" of the Oedipus complex. Repetition was the order of the day; the problem of psychotherapy was how to interrupt repetition, how to free up the future from its captivity by the past. Such a theory evolved in a society in which tradition was a powerful force, defining the limits of one's choices of occupation, mate, and place of residence. At the same time, there is a sense that tradition, the past, can become fixating, can become pathologically limiting of ongoing evolution. In the midst of tradition and change, people always need a degree of stability and predictability in their lives, as well as the flexibility and agility to respond to change, including unanticipated change. Functionality in the world of today and tomorrow seems to require a new balance between stability on one hand, and agility in responding to change on the other. In one respect at least, psychoanalytic theory appears to offer an apt framework: it pictures people as wanting to free themselves from fixations with the past that prevent flexibility and agility in moving forward into an unknown future. Now, with the future coming at us with such speed, our present is defined more by what we see coming, less by what we have come to know from the past. How are psychological theory and the practice of psychotherapy evolving to face this new future-oriented world?

Nonlinear dynamics in both developmental theory and in notions of psychotherapy practice seem to capture the present sense of a relatively unpredictable future. Smith and Thelen (1993) and Harris (2006) formulate nonlinear models of life-span development. Such models evolve from relational theories that acknowledge both the stages through which capacities and tendencies develop and the interpersonal environment with which individually derived stages interact. Children develop the capacity to speak, to think abstractly, to walk, and so on in a preprogrammed sequence, but interacting with an interpersonal and cultural environment that facilitates, obstructs, and shapes this developmental unfolding. An earlier focus on temperament and goodness of fit between child and parental temperamental factors (Chess & Thomas, 1996) was a forerunner of the focus on nonlinear factors and forces emerging from individual development as it interacting with an environment.

Psychotherapy process, too, has been conceptualized as evolving in a nonlinear fashion (Boston Change Process Study Group, 2010). Traditional notions of psychotherapy envisioned a therapist carrying out a technique in standardized fashion, with the patient responding in a relatively foreseeable fashion. Nonlinear theories of psychotherapy see the relationship as developing such that the interaction between therapist and patient develops systemic qualities, the system taking on a life of its own. The therapist's job is not only to carry out a predefined technique, but to keep an eye, as best he can, on the ripples created by his own actions influencing the patient as an individual as well as the system, which creates an infinite feedback loop. Relational psychoanalytic theory of technique (Mitchell, 1988; Aron,1996) similarly sees the psychoanalytic relationship as unfolding in nonlinear fashion in the course of emergent enactments. These enactments (i.e. the occurrence of conflictual patterns in the analytic relationship that reflect overlapping emotional hot spots for patient and analyst) develop out of an interaction between the preexisting internalized interpersonal expectations of each person emerging in the context of the actual interpersonal exchange and in the context of the psychoanalytic situation as it is set up by this particular dyad. Nonlinear notions of psychotherapy require of the therapist a kind of agility in responding to an unpredictable unfolding of events, reminiscent of the agility required currently of people as they face a fast-evolving and unpredictable future.

There are, in many fields of theory and human endeavor, cross currents and currents running upstream. In economic theory, there are one-dimensional linear theories such as those that assume that free markets always allocate resources most efficiently. Nonlinear dynamic systems theories posit unanticipated consequences from the operation of free markets such that regulations and intervention by government become necessary. These regulations and interventions in turn will have their own unanticipated consequences requiring further modifications.

In the fields of education and health, there is a one-dimensional, linear model of cost effectiveness applied to everything from psychotherapy to educational procedures from early childhood through graduate school. In psychotherapy, some authors are writing about complex, nonlinear dynamics in the psychotherapy relationship. At the same time, others are emphasizing measurable goals and objectives achievable in a short time frame. As a commodity, the more time consuming forms of psychotherapy based on complex, nonlinear models become the more expensive ones, available to those who can pay for more of it, while the short-term forms are the only ones available to those of limited financial means. Even here, however, the situation is not one-dimensional. There are many affluent people who want a simple and straightforward solution to problems of functionality, in fact, who speak no language other than the language of concrete problem solving. There are private practitioners with high fees who reserve some of their time for people who pay low fees, as well as training clinics in universities and training institutes where people are in intensive psychotherapy with trainees for extended periods for low fees. There are *pro bono* programs, such as New York's Fostering Connection and A Home Within around the United States, in which private practitioners therapy with people affected by foster care without a fee. These programs are efforts to imagine and put into practice psychotherapy outside the capitalist system, that is, to imagine psychotherapy as something other than a commodity. Such efforts to work outside the dominant system, however, have their own complexity and contradictions. The experience of trying to work outside the capitalist system provides an interesting case study of the interaction of individuals with systems at various levels.

## Psychotherapy Outside Capitalism?

Consider the term *pro bono*. The language implies that if one works for free, one must be doing so "for good." Is one to think, then, that those who work for a fee, or for a high fee, or the highest possible fee are doing so "for bad," that is, for greedy or other reprehensible motives? Is wanting a lot of money necessarily reprehensible? Does the moral status depend on what one wants the money for? Is a capitalistic system that rewards individual acquisitiveness morally bad, while a socialistic system that seeks economic equality or justice necessarily morally good?

A multidimensional, nonlinear look at these questions leads to the conclusion that motives are complex and contradictory on all levels from the individual to the large group. While socialism aimed at economic justice, the idea that there needed to be a dictatorship of the proletariat led to authoritarian, brutal, and violent Communist regimes. It took a long time for many on the political left in the United States and elsewhere in the West and around the world to acknowledge that the effort to transcend motives of economic self-interest did not automatically imply transcendence of political self-interest. In fact, it appears that those who have the most unquestioning belief in their own virtue, from the Crusaders to the Communists, are often those who feel entitled to commit, and do commit, the most abhorrent acts against those who oppose them or who have different values. This point is perhaps the most profound implication of Isaiah Berlin's (1969) idea that values are inherently in conflict and contradiction. Freedom and democracy, for example, do not go together, and in fact, cannot go together in principle. In order for the majority to prevail, the minority gives up some freedom. To avoid the tyranny of the majority, the majority must give up some freedom. There are various forms of freedom: freedom from interference and freedom to do what one wishes. An implication here is that the individual psychotherapist who offers his services without fee is not necessarily, or straightforwardly, doing so for "good." An article on this point (Altman, Bonovitz, Dunn, & Kandall, 2008) pointed out the complexities that arise when therapists present themselves to their patients as doing good. Many contemporary, analytically oriented therapists view the process as entailing an opportunity *within the relationship with the therapist* to rework negative templates of interpersonal interaction derived from bad early experiences. Presenting oneself as a "good" therapist (i.e., generous and nonexploitative) may work against evocation of the bad feelings associated with deprivation and exploitation that need to be addressed within the therapeutic relationship. The payment of fees in a psychotherapy relationship provides one opportunity for experiences of being deprived and exploited to arise. When there is no fee, this particular opportunity is ruled out. A challenge arises to integrate the "good" with other "bad," that is, depriving and exploitative experiences as they arise in the psychotherapy relationship. There is no shortage of such opportunities even when no fee is charged, some of which arise *because* no fee is charged. Offering free therapy does not mean a therapist will not try to make the patient pay with gratitude, appreciation, or by not being too demanding or too much "trouble." It does not mean she will not resent the more difficult or demanding parts of the patient with which she must cope without monetary recompense. It does not mean that she will not pat herself on her back for her goodness, that is, take narcissistic gratification in being so good and generous, indulging in rescue fantasies with all the condescension toward the patient that may entail. All these considerations are not reason *not* to do therapy *pro bono*, they are simply the "bad object" proclivities that go with doing therapy for no fee. But it is a good reason not to call therapy with no fee *pro bono*. It is also *pro malo*, or it is both or neither. The paradoxical point being made here is well captured by Hoffman (1998), who says that the generic good object is the one who is willing to be perceived by the patient as bad, while the generic bad object is the one who insists on being seen as good. Being depriving and exploitative, of course, in itself is only retraumatizing. But being *perceived* that way, with some degree of justification, at the same time as one has authentically good, generous intentions provides the opportunity for depressive position integration between good and bad with patients who have come to expect only bad from important people. Note that it is important that the therapist acknowledge that there is some degree of justification for the patients' view of her as depriving and exploitative, without invalidating her sense of self as a "helping" professional.

## Social/Political Implications

Returning to the large group, political level, we can now understand at least one of the reasons why so much damage is done by people who are convinced they are virtuous. The problem is in seeing oneself as *only* virtuous, since that entails both a refusal to see the ways one's good intentions are mixed with narcissistic and exploitative motives. It also leads to a need to attribute all such negative tendencies to others and to develop a scapegoat to hold all the badness. The problem with the Soviet Union was that it was unwilling to consider that the "dictatorship of the proletariat" would not only impose economic equality on people, but that it would fail to take account of the power hunger, if not economic hunger, that would be thus enabled. The problem with the United States, in the Cold War and at other times, is that it is too persuaded of its own virtue as a paragon of freedom and democracy, to the point where it can feel entitled to impose these virtues by force on others, or to seek out and hunt down those bad people (Communists) who oppose God-given freedom.

In a variety of ways, then, I am suggesting that there are many pitfalls to a linear approach—in child development, in psychotherapy, in politics and government—

when it is not balanced and complicated by a nonlinear systemic view. In that way, perhaps, I can be accused of smuggling in a linear perspective by being stubbornly of the opinion that linear points of view are wrong-headed and destructive. To this, I can accurately (in my view) and defensively respond that I am not *against* linear perspectives, only those that fail to integrate complexity and contradiction. In many cases, undoubtedly, I fail to acknowledge the degree to which people who present a fundamentally linear point of view (i.e., free markets work for the common good) recognize the relevant complexity (there is a correlated rise in income inequality, as well as a leveling of playing fields) that must be addressed. I recognize that the complexity and contradiction in this case is that I may be (somewhat) blind to my own smug satisfaction in having attained this more-complex-than-thou integration.

## The Commodification of Mindfulness

The Marxist idea of "alienation" refers to a process in which mindfulness is lost. When a person makes something, the person and the object produced are united in the process of production. In capitalism, money, an abstraction, stands between a person and the product of his work, especially when the product is sold by a third party (i.e., the owner of the means of production). The person, in the Marxist framework, is alienated from his own productivity, creativity, and his relationship to his world, as a relationship to money replaces the relationship to the thing produced in itself (see Kovel, 1989).

In Zen practice (Morita, 1998), mindfulness entails a parallel seamlessness in one's world. The person is at one with experience. In mindfulness meditation, distracting thoughts and feelings inevitably arise, but the goal is to encompass these, as well, in the integrated flow of experience. A process of alienation from oneself arises when one stands outside the flow of experience, objectifying it, opposing it, and observing it from a detached perspective.

Chogyam Trungpa (1973), a Tibetan Buddhist teacher, reflecting on a process he called "spiritual materialism," observed that sometimes one's efforts to transcend ego can become, paradoxically and perversely, the cause for inflated narcissism. In this view, narcissism, or what the Buddhists call "ego" (as opposed to the psychoanalytic concept of ego) is a wily thing, insinuating itself even into the process of transcending it, requiring constant vigilance on the part of the spiritual practitioner.

What Trungpa called "spiritual materialism" bears a resemblance to what Ghent (1990, 1992) spoke of as false self look-alikes of true self processes. In one example, he spoke of masochistic submission as a false self-camouflage for the process of surrender of false self. False self look-alikes serve a defensive function. For example, when surrender seems to entail too much vulnerability, one might seek out opportunities to submit masochistically as a way of seeming to surrender while the deeper wish to surrender remains hidden, cloaked in ritualized sexual enactments. The longing and the defense against it are each made manifest in a paradoxical form in relation to each other.

Similarly, when mindfulness threatens to bring people too close to an anxiety-provoking awareness of transience or to other anxiety-producing aspects of experience, people may seek an experience of mindfulness cloaked in antimindfulness (i.e., an objectifying state of mind).

## Mental Health Systems in the Context of Global Capitalism

One program in the South Bronx area of New York City has traditionally served over three thousand chronic psychiatric patients. Recently, with cuts to Medicaid funding, the number of visits per year for which the program can be reimbursed has been cut to thirty, twelve of which are set aside for psychiatric visits to review medication treatment. Subsequent visits after the thirty mark is reached are reimbursed at a lower rate for a certain number of visits and further reduced after that number is exceeded. In short, chronic psychiatric patients, prone to suicidal and homicidal impulses and psychotic thinking, are allocated only eighteen psychotherapy visits per year at full rate. Continuing care is often offered to high-risk patients at increasingly reduced rates over the course of the year.

Current priorities in the New York State government emphasize that mentally ill people are more likely to neglect their physical health. They then develop conditions such as diabetes and asthma, and other predisposing conditions such as obesity, that are costly to the system. Thus, it happens that losing weight becomes a priority in setting goals and objectives for mentally ill people, with mental health clinicians expected to have a scale in their offices to weigh patients at each visit. In general, the priorities of the New York State Office of Mental Health, on the basis of which it supports public mental health clinics, is that community-based support offered to chronic patients will reduce relatively expensive emergency room visits and inpatient treatment for both psychiatric and physical conditions. It is difficult to imagine how such goals could realistically be accomplished given the severe restrictions imposed on outpatient visits and given that there is no provision for funding home visits to monitor treatment compliance. If a patient whose allocated visits are exhausted becomes suicidal or homicidal or otherwise absolutely requires treatment, the clinic is caught between providing unreimbursed treatment and unethically turning away someone who is dangerous to himself or others. The system seems set up to abandon, nearly completely, this most marginalized of populations, the poverty-stricken chronically mentally ill of color. The language and ideology of short-term behavioral psychotherapy is appropriated to rationalize and justify a "treatment" approach whereby goals should be able to be met simply because the goal is set, not because a realistic plan has been thoughtfully put in place and funded. It would be expensive and time consuming to provide public funding to plan and implement an approach including the occasional hospitalization, medication, talk-therapy sessions, and home visits necessary realistically to stabilize this group of people. On the other hand, one must consider the cost of not acknowledging their existence and needs. In the 1960s, such people were hospitalized long-term at great cost in public funding. As noted previously, they were "de-institutionalized" with much fanfare, released to the "community" with a plan for community-based mental health services at a fraction of the cost of hospitalization. When community mental health was downsized or eliminated to save money, these people ended up homeless, living on the streets or in publicly funded shelters. A huge crisis of homelessness ensued, with high crime and drug abuse rates. The solution proposed for this problem in the 1970s, with so-called Rockefeller laws, was to imprison people for minor drug crimes, in some cases (on the third conviction) for long sentences. Three strikes and you're out, out of sight and out of mind. Then it turns out it's even more expensive to imprison people than it is to hospitalize them, especially when prisoners become the largest group of mentally ill people in the United States (Kupers, 1999). As of this writing, the strategy is to overturn the "Rockefeller" drug laws and to set free many prisoners, at the same time as there is decreased funding to provide follow-up mental health services for them. In one way or another, as a society, we seem to be trying to blind ourselves to the existence of the chronically mentally ill people in our midst. In the language of psychoanalysis, this is called "denial," one of the least adaptive defense mechanisms. We misuse treatments (medication and short-term behavioral treatments) to support our denial, seizing the promise they seem to offer of inexpensive cure, or at least management. Meanwhile, the chronically mentally ill, like the poor, do not go away, while those on the front lines who are supposed to pick up the pieces with few resources or support become increasingly demoralized, and the society itself increasingly dehumanized.

## Portugal

"What would you do if you were the Prime Minister of Portugal?" I asked Miguel Moita, whose program to serve disruptive children in the public schools in Portugal had just been abruptly shut down due to budget cuts. "I would first tell the people that we had to do things that would entail losing our souls." Taken aback, I struggled for words. "You mean, if there was no way out from closing programs like yours, at least we should call what was happening by its right name?" "Right," he replied. Moita acknowledged that Portugal had a real economic crisis because the government had borrowed too much money in the previous decades. It was now paralyzed by interest and repayment costs. The solution to this problem proposed by the European Union, dominated by Germany, and the International Monetary Fund (IMF), dominated by the United States, was austerity, and that meant shrinking the public sector. He continued, "We cannot accept that the choice we are facing is either to be part of a politics of continuous growth through the full satisfaction of the demands of the markets or else to be in some kind of an abyss. This politics is creating endless suffering for much of the Portuguese people and is now being borne by the twenty percent of the population in Portugal who are unemployed, and the more than fifty percent of people under twenty-five who are unemployed. We must come up with a more humane response to the economic crisis. Portugal cannot stay still while facing the official discourse that we have no alternatives, and must get ready to subvert this view, and protect our people possibly through a new sustainable model focusing on human wellbeing rather than economic growth."

On my visit to Portugal to speak at a conference on "Violence and Evil," sponsored by the Portuguese local chapter of the International Association for Relational Psychoanalysis and Psychotherapy, I heard a number of times a determination to take psychoanalysis out of its insular location in the private office and make it relevant to the social and economic pain now gripping the nation. Earlier, the previous month, at the semiannual conference of the International Association for Relational Psychoanalysis and Psychotherapy in Santiago, Chile, I had been struck by how many of the plenary talks had focused on the recent violent history of Chile, going back to the dispossession of the native population by the Spanish colonists.

Moita's program ("Pensamento Vivo," or "Living Thought") began in 2010 in response to a crisis in the public education system in Portugal. After a finding by the European Commission that child labor existed in Portugal, the government moved to make sure that children were attending school. As a result, the schools had to accommodate large numbers of new students who were not accustomed to going to school. Many of them, of course, had learning problems. They also had to be brought up to speed academically. In many cases, they posed behavioral problems for the school authorities. The solution was to segregate such children in special schools. After being isolated from the larger society by being out of school, according to Moita, they were now isolated from their age mates in school.

Moita began a program in one school to consult to the teachers and to see some of the disruptive children in psychotherapy groups. He applied for government funding and was awarded a large grant to establish programs in many locations in Portugal to consult to the teachers in groups. He hired people to see some children individually and in groups in order to help integrate formerly out-of-school children into the mainstream schools.

Just before my visit to Lisbon in late 2013, the staff of Moita's program arrived at work one morning to find that the program had been closed down overnight because of budget cuts. Children, teachers, and staff were not informed ahead of time. There was no time to discuss the need to end their work together and the emotional reactions of the participants. Whatever work toward processing emotions had been done in this program was abruptly undone by a system that, as Moita put it, had "lost its soul."

Moita's statement (personal communication, December 1, 2013) about acknowledging that Portugal was losing its soul, even if there seemed to be no options, reflected a particular ethic: an ethic of responsibility, of truth telling about loss and pain, of tolerance of guilt, and of holding onto what has been lost through memory and naming. Naming and taking responsibility for inhumane treatment of those who suffer is an antidote to phenomena like internalized racism and the "hidden injuries of class" (Sennett & Cobb, 1972) by which people come to blame themselves for their own oppression and deprivation. It acts as an antidote to a dynamic described by Ferenczi (1949) whereby children who are sexually abused take on the guilt of the perpetrator in cases where the perpetrator mystifies the child by denying that anything exploitative and damaging is occurring.

## The United States

Cushman (in press), citing the Congressional Research Service (2012), Mishel, Bivens, Gould, and Shierholz (2012), and Piketty and Saez (2003) documents that economic inequality in the United States has reached levels not seen since the Great Depression. At the same time, there have been massive cuts to social programs (Kupers, 1990; Linden, 2010; McNichol, 2012) so that those at the bottom have less support. In particular, community-based mental health systems, according to Cushman (in press), citing Honberg, Diehl, Kimball, Gruttadaro, and Fitzpatrick (2011), are increasingly underfunded at a time when demand for these services is increasing. As noted above, funders demand short-term "evidence based" techniques with stringent requirements for documentation of effectiveness on a short-term basis in order to maintain funding. At a time when people are under increasing stress from economic pressure, the support available to them is decreasing. Meanwhile, service providers are expected to "cure" the fallout from ever-increasing social neglect with shrinking resources. It is as if our society says to the mentally ill, "Medical treatment will be available to you as long as your symptoms can be demonstrated to result from strictly physiological sources within your skin, disconnected from the social, economic, and political realities with which you have to cope. If your problems are significantly economic or political, you are on your own to improve your station in life." From a perspective that regards use of public services as a negative factor for mental health (i.e., as encouraging dysfunctional dependency), being left on one's own may be seen as a kind of plus for mental health. It might also be argued that shrinking the public sector will lead to a vigorous private sector that can produce jobs that will be good for peoples' mental health. On the other hand, for those who see public services as part of a social ethos in which we are all responsible for each other and for the wellbeing of our communities, who believe that the use of public services, including mental health services, does not necessarily encourage dependence, or that dependence when seen as part of interdependence is not a bad thing, this is a toxic "perfect storm." It is bad for the mental health of those on the lower end of the economic scale, indeed for all of us. It is toxic for the United States, the world as a community, and for those of us in the mental health professions who believe that psychological work with anyone, particularly those who are deeply disturbed, is a complicated and sometimes time-consuming process. Those on the lower end of the economic scale are actually the great majority of people in a society with inequality as great as that which exists in the United States. Advocacy by mental health organizations has recently led to laws requiring wider coverage for mental health treatment by insurance companies, regardless of the cost of the plan. Publicly funded mental health services, or private services funded by insurance companies, however, are under great pressure to keep services time limited, with a focus on quantifiable results. The net result is that, one way or the other, psychotherapy that is responsive to the complexity of peoples' lives is available only to those at the higher end of the economic continuum. At the same time, clinicians are subject to the same economic and psychological pressures as everyone else, so, in global capitalism, those of us who are clinicians will tend to gravitate toward high fee private practice when we can. The system by which the majority of people are left out of high quality work thus appears self-perpetuating. It is difficult, but not impossible, to see a way out.

A way out may consist of keeping in mind that income inequality is bad for the mental health of those at the upper end of the economic scale, as well as for those at the bottom. Under the current regime, those of us who want to advocate for public mental health services cannot make the self-interest of the economically and politically privileged our adversary. We need, rather, an expanded vision of what self-interest consists of, beyond economic and political power. Wachtel (1989) and Altman (2004) have pointed out the price paid in insecurity by the affluent for the overemphasis on the kind of security obtained through material possessions. Piff, Stancato, Martinez, Kraus, and Keltner (2012) and Piff (2013) also demonstrate that upper class status can conduce to narcissism in various forms. Narcissism was defined by Piff (2013) as a sense of undue entitlement (manifested in selfishness), reduced sensitivity to the suffering of others, and self-serving unethical and illegal behavior. From the point of view of a materialistic value system, such behavior may (or may not) pay off, but from the point of view of a communitarian value system, there is a price to be paid, often by one's significant others. As noted above, Baldwin's (1993) work is eloquent testimony to the price paid in dehumanization by those caught on the treadmill of security seeking through wealth and power.

Stiglitz (2003) describes and explains, with the insight of an economist, the global capitalist system that has led to the shrinking public sector noted here. According to Stiglitz, in the wake of the Great Depression and World War II, a global system was set up to support the economies of the world in the cyclic downturns endemic to capitalism. Under the influence of Keynsian economics, the dominant idea was that when economies are in a state of contraction, government spending should be increased to raise demand for goods and services to stimulate the economy. The IMF and the World Bank were set up to loan money to countries with distressed economies in the interest of stimulating growth.

In the Reagan-Thatcher years of the 1980s, however, the dominant theory changed by 180 degrees: the idea then was that economies function best under "free market" conditions, i.e., without government intervention or interference. In that case, shrinking economies were understood to result from government interference with the workings of the free market. When the IMF and the World Bank loaned money to countries with distressed economies, the funds came with the requirement that government spending must decrease, with increased openness to foreign investment, free international flow of capital, and reduced or eliminated barriers to international trade. All of this in the interest of free markets.

Stiglitz documents the one-two punch this prescription delivered to economically poor people around the world. On one hand, support for those in poverty was reduced as government spending resulted in a shrinking public sector, as I have noted with respect to mental health funding at many points in this book. On the other hand, the free entry of multinational corporations into economically distressed economies resulted in considerable job loss for those employed by pre-existing local businesses before retraining programs and temporary support for the unemployed could be set up. Farmers now had to compete with heavily subsidized farmers in the United States and elsewhere in the world to sell their crops in a global market (ironically and tragically, while the United States-dominated IMF required that governments in economically distressed countries reduce interference with the functioning of free markets, United States farmers continued to be subsidized by their government, allowing them to sell their crops more cheaply than was possible for unsubsidized farmers). Free flow of capital brought boom and bust cycles to Asia, Latin America, and Africa as currency speculators in New York and London moved money in and out of various currencies, often in response to rumors, creating stampedes in and out.

Stiglitz maintains that global free markets have the potential to benefit economically poor people around the world by creating new jobs and markets, but that these reforms must be cultivated at a pace slow enough to allow for support of those who are temporarily or permanently displaced or thrown into a global market at a disadvantage. A one-dimensional linear view that free markets automatically and immediately benefit everyone, in reality, only benefits the multinational corporations, while in the short run, the economically disadvantaged are hurt. The rich get richer and the poor get poorer. A system of austerity is imposed by governments in the United States and Europe, with enormous consequences in Asia, Africa, and Latin America, without political responsibility to the people whose lives are affected. This is why the current global economic system can be fairly termed "neo-colonial."

# Chapter 8

# Conclusion and Prospects

Our world is changing at a dizzying pace. To an unprecedented degree, each of us is on our own, with less support from tradition, from family, from employers, and from the public sector. At the same time, the skills necessary to keep our heads above water economically keep changing. The education we received last year or last decade may not be relevant to what we will need to stay afloat tomorrow. We expect more from our relationships, yet have more and more difficulty meeting people. Seemingly paradoxically, the culture seems to be moving toward one-dimensional concerns with cost effectiveness and clearly definable goals and objectives for our work, as if we could or should know where we are going. Of course, there really is no contradiction. When we are frightened and confused, we look for some foundation, something to believe in, some assurance that things are under control, or at least could be under control. When things are too predictable, when tradition tells us too clearly who we are and how to live our lives, we feel constrained and look for freedom, risk, and the unpredictable. When things are too unpredictable, again we long for stability and knowability. We swing back and forth, continually getting too much of what we had hoped for. For now, change seems here to stay, as does the longing for stability.

Psychoanalysis evolved at a time when tradition in Europe was breaking down, when individualism was on the rise. Psychoanalysis took tradition and made it into an internal force, an internalized superego. Conflict between the individual's self-interested desires and the requirements of tradition became an internal conflict that could be mediated and resolved through the rational offices of the ego. The idea of the unconscious, however, was a far more radical notion that speaks well to our current situation. The notion of the unconscious undermines whatever we think we know about ourselves. Self-knowledge becomes tentative, subject to being undermined by its opposite. We contain repressed aspects of ourselves, dissociated self-states, parts of ourselves with which we are not familiar, parts we would wish to disavow and deny. This sense of flux and contradiction in human life and consciousness suits well the present moment of uncertainty and change. But just as living in a time of rapid unpredictable change gives rise for longings for stability, the destabilizing elements of psychoanalysis are profoundly out of synch with the current cultural desire for stability and predictability. Psychoanalysis comes to be defined as a nonempirically validated treatment, as if we knew how to define clearly what we want and how to get it. The core message of psychoanalysis is that we do not know what we want. Consumer capitalism takes advantage of this uncertainty, and the unease it engenders, to try to convince us that our desires can be defined, and then met with products. In this context, psychoanalysis is profoundly, radically disruptive and unwelcome.

Capitalism can transform anything, including psychoanalysis, into a product to be sold. Psychoanalysts, perhaps inevitably, have come to see what they have to offer as an upscale commodity, for an exclusive clientele, with prices to match. But, psychoanalysis has a branding problem. It does not promise to make us happy in any simple or straightforward way. By embracing the medical framework, defining itself as a medical specialty, it ties itself to a model of symptom relief that feeds straight into the empirically validated treatment movement. Psychoanalysis, as medical specialty, is at odds with itself as a critical force in society. In a capitalist cultural context, the timelessness of a psychoanalytic session or a psychoanalytic treatment becomes a reckless disregard for the fact that time is money.

After World War II, especially in the United States, psychoanalysts, in search of material privilege, turned away from the public sector with its economic poverty and associated problems. In recent decades, as public sector budgets shrink, the public sector has turned away from psychoanalysis. Public health falls within the province of public funding, so accountability in terms of cost effectiveness is an especially crucial issue in the public sector. The economically poor who depend on public funding for their services are especially vulnerable to the impact of considerations of cost effectiveness. Children of the economically poor are far more likely to be taught in a way designed to raise their scores on high stakes tests, as in "No Child Left Behind," much more so than the children of the economically affluent who are more likely to be taught in a way that promotes creativity and individual initiative. The children of the economically affluent are prepared for the unpredictable, fast changing world of the modern economy, while the children of the economically poor are prepared to follow directions, to learn by rote, for whatever place in the future economy that requires those capacities. The economically poor are more likely to have their psychological problems treated with medication and short-term psychotherapy designed to reduce the economic burden of their problems and symptoms on society. The economically affluent have more degrees of freedom, since they pay for themselves. At one stroke, free market ideology results in policies that enrich corporate shareholders, reduce the services available to the already disadvantaged while making a one-dimensional notion of cost effectiveness the criterion for what is worthwhile, a criterion from which the affluent can be exempt.

The world remains a complex, contradictory place. Complex-minded perspectives like psychoanalysis are likely to speak to our experience on individual and social levels from however marginalized a place. Short-term, evidence-based treatments are to psychoanalysis as one-size-fits-all free market solutions are to the complex mix of markets with government regulation and intervention that seems necessary to manage globalization's non-linear development and unanticipated consequences. Psychoanalysis has a history of capitalizing on unanticipated consequences to learn something new (recall how Freud discovered transference in Anna O.'s unanticipated love for Breuer). The unconscious keeps individuals continually off balance, seeking some sort of footing, like the contemporary world with its disorienting pace of change.

One unanticipated consequence of globalization and free market ideology has been the dehumanization of the public sphere along with the marginalization of psychoanalysis itself. But psychoanalysts have not faced up to the challenge of this situation because: a) the social domain is ruled out of bounds for psychoanalysis by many psychoanalysts, and/or b) some analysts have an economically vested interest in the status quo. The potential of psychoanalysis to challenge itself appeals to me still, indeed, all the more; I hope to have stimulated some interest in self-examination with this book.

# References

Agarwal, A. (2013) A roadmap for energy security. In: C. Chandler & A. Zainulbhai (Eds.), *Reimagining India* (pp. 254–257). New York: Simon and Schuster.

Ahern, A. E. (1978) Sacred and secular medicine in a Taiwan village: a study of cosmological disorders. In: A. Kleinman, P. Kunstadter, E. R. Alexander, & J. L. Gayle (Eds.), *Culture and Healing in Asian Societies* (pp. 91–114). Cambridge, MA: Schenkman.

Ainslie, R. C. (1995) *No Dancin' in Anson: An American Story of Race and Social Change.* Northvale, NJ and London: Jason Aronson.

Ainslie, R. C. (1999) *Crossover.* Dos Manos Productions, LLC.

Ainslie, R. C. (2002–2006) Jasper, Texas: The healing of a community in crisis (in collaboration with photographer Sarah Wilson). A photographic exhibit shown in various cities.

Ainslie, R. C. (2004) *Long Dark Road: Bill King and Murder in Jasper, Texas.* Austin, TX: University of Texas Press.

Ainslie, R. C. (Dir.) (2006) *Looking North: Mexican Images of Immigration* [documentary film]. Austin, TX: Dos Manos Productions.

Ainslie, R. C. (Dir.) (2007) *Ya Basta!* [documentary film]. Austin, TX: Dos Manos Productions.

Ainslie, R. C. (2013a) *The Fight to Save Juarez.* Austin, TX: University of Texas Press.

Ainslie, R. C. (2013b) Intervention strategies for addressing collective trauma: Healing communities ravaged by racial strife. *Psychoanalysis, Culture and Society* 18(2): 140–152.

Ainsworth, M.D.S. (1963) The development of infant-mother interaction among the Ganda. In: B. M. Foss (Ed.), *Determinants of Infant Behavior* (pp. 67–104). New York: Wiley.

Ainsworth, M.D.S. (1967) *Infancy in Uganda: Infant Care and the Growth of Love.* Baltimore: Johns Hopkins University Press.

Ainsworth, M.D.S., Blehar, M. C., Waters, E., & Walls, S. (1978) *Patterns of Attachment: A Psychological Study of the Strange Situation.* Hillsdale, NJ: Erlbaum.

Alliance of Psychoanalytic Organizations. (2006) *Psychodynamic Diagnostic Manual.* New York: American Psychoanalytic Association.

Alpert, J. (1995) *Psychological Consultation in Educational Settings: Casebook for Working with Administrators, Teachers, Students, and Community.* Northvale, NJ: Jason Aronson.

Altman, N. (2004) Manic society: Toward the depressive position. *Psychoanalytic Dialogues* 15(3): 321–346.

Altman, N. (2010) *The Analyst in the Inner City: Race, Class, and Culture Through a Psychoanalytic Lens.* London and New York: Routledge.

Altman, N., Bonovitz, C., Dunn, K., & Kandall, E. (2008) On being bad while doing good. *Journal of Infant, Child, and Adolescent Psychotherapy* 7(1): 14–36.

Aron, L. (1996) *A Meeting of Minds*. Hillsdale, NJ: The Analytic Press.

Aron, L., & Starr, K. (2012) *A Psychotherapy for the People*. London and New York: Routledge.

Baldwin, J. (1993) *The Fire Next Time*. New York: Vintage International.

Bandura, A. (1990) Selective activation and disengagement of moral control. *Journal of Social Issues* 46(1): 27–46.

Becker, E. (1973) *The Denial Of Death*. New York: Free Press.

Benjamin, J. (2001) The primal leap of psychoanalysis, from body to speech: Freud, feminism, and the vicissitudes of the transference. In: M. Dimen & A. Harris (Eds.), *Storms in Her Head: Freud and the Construction of Hysteria* (pp. 31–64). New York: Other Press.

Berlin, I. (1969) *Four Essays on Liberty*. Oxford: Oxford University Press.

Bertrand, A. (1826) Extase. In: A.J.F. Bertrand (Ed.), *Encyclopedie Progressive* (pp. 337–392). Paris: Bureau de l'encyclopedie progressive.

Bion, W.R.D. (1988) Attacks on linking. In: E. Bott-Spillius (Ed.), *Melanie Klein Today Volume 1* (pp. 87–101). London: Routledge.

Bolding, E. (2005) *Before and After N. Dorgenois*. New Orleans, LA, and Brooklyn, NY: Red Rattle Books/Soft Skull Press.

Boston Change Process Study Group. (2010) *Change in Psychotherapy: A Unifying Paradigm*. New York: Norton.

Bowlby, J. (1969) *Attachment and Loss: Volume 1, Attachment*. New York: Basic Books.

Bowlby, J. (1973) *Attachment and Loss: Volume 2, Separation: Anxiety and Anger*. New York: Basic Books.

Bowlby, J. (1980) *Attachment and Loss: Volume 3, Loss: Sadness and Depression*. New York: Basic Books.

Bragin, M. (2004) The uses of aggression: Healing the wounds of war in a community context. In: B. Sklarew, S. Twemlow, & S. Wilkinson (Eds.), *Analysts in the Trenches: Streets, Schools, and War Zones* (pp. 169–194). Hillsdale, NJ: The Analytic Press.

Breuer, J. (1955) Anna O. In: J. Strachey (Ed.), *Freud S. The Standard Edition of the Complete Psychological Works of Sigmund Freud, Volume 2* (pp. 21–47). London, Hogarth Press.

Breuer, J., & Freud, S. (1893–1895) Studies on hysteria. In: J. Strachey (Ed.), *Standard Edition of the Complete Psychological Works of Sigmund Freud Volume 2* (pp. 1–311). London: Hogarth Press.

Brickman, C. (2003) *Aboriginal Populations in the Mind: Race and Primitivity in Psychoanalysis*. New York: Teachers College Press.

Bromberg, P. (1998) *Standing in the Spaces: Essays on Clinical Process, Trauma, & Dissociation*. Hillsdale, NJ: The Analytic Press.

Bromberg, P. (2001) Hysteria, dissociation, and cure. In: M. Dimen & A. Harris (Eds.), *Storms in Her Head: Freud and the Construction of Hysteria* (pp. 121–142). New York: Other Press.

Bührmann, M. V. (1984) *Living in Two Worlds*. Cape Town and Pretoria: Human and Rousseau.

Castano, E., & Giner-Sorolla, R. (2006) Not quite human: Dehumanization in response to responsibility for intergroup killing. *Journal of Personality and Social Psychology* 90: 804–818.

Chess, S., & Thomas, A. (1996) *Temperament*. New York and London: Routledge.

Congressional Research Service. (2012) Taxes and the economy: An economic analysis of the top tax rates since 1945. (CRS report number R42729). Retrieved from http://www.nytimes.com/news/business/0915taxesandeconomy.pdf

Cregeen, S. (2008) Workers, groups, and gangs: Consultation to residential adolescent teams. *Journal of Child Psychotherapy* 34(2): 172–189.

Curry, E. (2005) *The Road to Whatever: Middle Class Culture and the Crisis of Adolescence.* New York: Macmillan.

Cushman, D. (in press) Case management and the analytic frame: A new paradigm. *fort da.*

Cushman, P. (1995) *Constructing the Self, Constructing America.* New York: Addison-Wesley.

Danto, E. A. (2005) *Freud's Free Clinics: Psychoanalysis and Social Justice 1918–1938.* New York: Teachers College Press.

Darwin, J. (2012) Strategic outreach to families of all reservists. In: N. D. Ainspan & W.E. Penk (Eds.), *When the Warrior Returns: Making the Transition at Home.* Annapolis, MD: Naval Institute Press.

Deleuze, G., & Guattari, F. (1983) *Anti Oedipus: Capitalism and Schizophrenia.* Minneapolis: University of Minnesota Press.

Doi, T. L. (1962) Morita therapy and psychoanalysis. *Psychologia* 5(3): 117–123.

Dunn, A. J. (2012) Contractual based school psychotherapy. *Journal of Infant, Child, and Adolescent Psychotherapy* 11(3): 284–296.

Emmanuel, L. (2002) Deprivation X3: The contribution of organizational dynamics to the "triple deprivation" of looked-after children. *Journal of Child Psychotherapy* 28(2): 163–179.

Ewing, K. P. (1998) A Mazjub and his mother: The place of sainthood in a family's emotional memory. In: P. Werbner & H. Basu (Eds.), *Embodying Charisma: Modernity, Locality, and the Performance of Emotion in Sufi Cults* (pp. 160–183). London and New York: Routledge.

Fairbairn, W.R.D. (1958) The nature and aims of psychoanalytic treatment. *International Journal of Psychoanalysis* 39: 374–385.

Fanon, F. (1963) *The Wretched of the Earth.* New York: Grove Press.

Farley, A. J., & Manning, D. (2002) A three tiered, applied psychoanalytic intervention to support young children's emotional development. *Journal of Applied Psychoanalytic Studies* 4(3): 303–316.

Ferenczi, S. (1949) Confusion of tongues between the adults and the child (the language of tenderness and of passion). *International Journal of Psychoanalysis* 30: 225–230.

Flynn, D. (1998) Psychoanalytic Aspects of Inpatient Treatment. *Journal of Child Psychotherapy* 24(2): 283–306.

Fraiberg, S., Adelson, E., & Shapiro, V. (1975) Ghosts in the nursery: a psychoanalytic approach to the problem of impaired mother-infant relationships. *Journal of Child Psychiatry* 14: 387–421.

Frembgen, W. F. (1998) The Majzub Mama Ji Sarkar 'A friend of God moves from one house to another'. In: P. Werbner & H. Basu (Eds.), *Embodying Charisma: Modernity, Locality, and the Performance of Emotion in Sufi Cults* (pp. 140–159). London and New York: Routledge.

Freud, A., & Burlingham, D. (1943) *Infants Without Families.* London: G. Allen and Unwin.

Freud, S. (1901) The Interpretation of Dreams. In: J. Strachey (Ed.), *Standard Edition of the Complete Psychological Works of Sigmund Freud Volumes 4 and 5.* London: Hogarth Press.

Freud, S. (1905) *Dora: An Analysis of a Case of Hysteria.* NY: Touchstone Books. Republished 1963.

Freud, S. (1912) The dynamics of transference. In: J. Strachey (Ed.), *Standard Edition of the Complete Psychological Works of Sigmund Freud Volume 12* (pp. 97–108). London: Hogarth Press.

Freud, S. (1913) *Totem and Taboo.* In: J. Strachey (Ed.), *The Standard Edition of the Complete Psychological Works of Sigmund Freud Volume 13* (pp. 1–100). London: Hogarth Press.

Freud, S. (1914) On the history of the psychoanalytic movement. In: J. Strachey (Ed.), *Standard Edition of the Complete Psychological Works of Sigmund Freud Volume 14* (pp. 1–66). London: Hogarth Press.

Freud, S. (1915) The Unconscious. In: J. Strachey (Ed.), *Standard Edition of the Complete Psychological Works of Sigmund Freud Volume 14* (pp. 159–215). London: Hogarth Press.

Freud, S. (1919) Lines of advance in psychoanalytic therapy. In: J. Strachey (Ed.), *The Standard Edition of the Complete Psychological Works of Sigmund Freud Volume 17* (pp. 157–168). London: Hogarth Press. Republished in 1955.

Freud, S. (1925) Some additional notes on dream interpretation as a whole. In: J. Strachey (Ed.), *Standard Edition of the Complete Psychological Works of Sigmund Freud Volume 19* (pp. 123–138). London: Hogarth Press.

Freud, S. (1926) The question of lay analysis. In: J. Strachey (Ed.), *Standard Edition of the Complete Psychological Worlds of Sigmund Freud Volume 20* (pp. 179–258). London: Hogarth Press.

Freud, S. (2002) *Civilization and its Discontents.* London: Penguin. Originally published 1930.

Fromm, E. (1947) *Man For Himself.* Greenwich, CT: Fawcett.

Gabbard, G. (1986) Treatment of the "special" patient in a psychoanalytic hospital. *International Review of Psychoanalysis* 13: 333–347.

Gadamer, H-G. (1975) *Truth and Method.* New York: Crossroads.

Gay, P. (1987) *A Godless Jew: Freud, Atheism, and the Making of Psychoanalysis.* New Haven: Yale University Press.

Ghent, E. (1990) Masochism, submission, and surrender. *Contemporary Psychoanalysis* 28: 108–136.

Ghent, E. (1992) Paradox and process. *Psychoanalytic Dialogues* 2(2): 135–159.

Gilman, S. (1993) *Freud, Race, and Gender.* Princeton, NJ: Princeton University Press.

Goldstein, J. (2001) The case history in historical perspective: Nanette Leroux and Emmy von N. In: M. Dimen & A. Harris (Eds.), *Storms in Her Head: Freud and the Construction of Hysteria* (pp. 143–166). New York: Other Press.

Greenberg, J., Solomon, S., & Pyszczynski, T. (1997) Terror management theory of self esteem and cultural world views: Empirical assessments and conceptual refinements. In: P. M. Zanna (Ed.), *Advances in Experimental Social Psychology Volume 29* (pp. 61–139). San Diego: Academic Press, Inc.

Grossmann, K., Grossmann, K. E., Spangler, G., Suess, G., & Unzner, L. (1985) Maternal sensitivity and newborns' orientation responses as related to quality of attachment in northern Germany. *Monographs for the Society for Research in Child Development* 50(1–2): 233–256.

Harrington, A. (1988) Hysteria, hypnosis, and the lure of the invisible: The rise of neo-Mesmerism in fin-de-siecle French Psychiatry. In: W. F. Bynum, R. Porter, & M. Shepherd (Eds.), *The Anatomy of Madness: Essays in the History of Psychiatry Volume 3 The Asylum and its Psychiatry.* New York: Routledge.

Harrington, A., Ed. (1997) *The Placebo Effect: An Interdisciplinary Exploration.* Cambridge, MA: Harvard University Press.

Harris, A. (2006) *Gender as Soft Assembly.* Hillsdale, NJ: The Analytic Press.

Hegel, G. (1977) *Phenomonology of Spirit.* A. V. Miller (Trans.). London: Oxford University Press. Original work published 1807.

Hegel, G. (2006) *Lectures on the Philosophy of Religion, Together with a Work on the Proofs of the Existence of God, by Georg Wilhelm Friedrich Hegel.* E. G. Spiers & J. Burdon Sanderson (Trans.). Routledge and Kegan Paul. Original work published 1895.

Hoffman, I. Z. (1998) *Ritual and Spontaneity in Psychoanalysis.* Hillsdale, NJ: The Analytic Press.

Hoffman, M. (2010) *Toward Mutual Recognition: Relational Psychoanalysis and the Christian Narrative.* New York and London: Routledge.

Holmes, E. (1995) Educational intervention for young children who have experienced fragmented care. In: J. Trowell & M. Bower (Eds.), *The Emotional Needs of Young Children and Their Families: Using Psychoanalytic Ideas in the Community* (pp. 148–156). London and New York: Routledge.

Holmes, J. (2012) A model of intervention at a psychoanalytic parent/child drop-in group in a poor district of Lima, Peru. *Journal of Child Psychotherapy* 38(2): 170–184.

Honberg, R., Diehl, S., Kimball, A., Gruttadaro, D., & Fitzpatrick, M. (2011) State mental health cuts: A national crisis. Retrieved from National Alliance on Mental Illness: http://www.nami.org/ContentManagement/ContentDisplay.cfm?ContentFileID=126233

Ignatiev, N. (1993) *How the Irish Became White.* London: Routledge.

Indian Psychoanalytic Society. (1999) *The Beginnings of Psychoanalysis in India: Bose-Freud Correspondence.* Calcutta: G.M. Enterprises.

Jacobs, L. (2012) Assessment as consultation: Working with parents and teachers. *Journal of Infant, Child, and Adolescent Psychotherapy* 11(3): 257–271.

Jaques, E. (1955) Social systems as defence against persecutory and depressive anxiety. In: M. Klein, P. Heinemann, & R. E. Money Kyrle (Eds.), *New Directions in Psycho-Analysis* (pp. 478–498). Tavistock: London.

Jung, C. G. (1954) The development of personality. In: G. Adler & R.F.C. Hull (Eds.), *Collected Works of C.G. Jung Volume 17.* Princeton, NJ: Princeton University Press.

Kakar, S. (1982) *Shamans, Mystics, and Doctors.* Chicago, IL: University of Chicago Press.

Kakar, S. (1997) Encounters of the psychological kind: Freud, Jung and India. In: *Culture and Psyche: Psychoanalysis and India* (pp. 20–30). New York: Psyche Press.

Kakar, S. (2008) *Culture and Psyche.* Second Edition. Oxford: Oxford University Press.

Kernberg, O. (1995) An interview with Otto Kernberg. *Psychoanalytic Dialogues: The International Journal of Relational Perspectives* 5(2): 325–349.

Kiev, A. (1972) *Transcultural Psychiatry.* New York: The Free Press.

Klein, M. (1975) *Envy and Gratitude.* New York: Delacorte Press/Seymour Lawrence.

Kleinman, A. (1991) *Rethinking Psychiatry: From Cultural Category to Personal Experience.* New York: Free Press.

Kleinman, A., Kunstadter, P., Alexander, E. R., & Gayle, J. L., Eds. (1978) *Culture and Healing in Asian Societies.* Cambridge, MA: Schenkman.

Kovel, J. (1989) *The Radical Spirit: Essays in Psychoanalysis and Society.* London: Free Association Books.

Kraemer, S. (2006) So the cradle won't fall: Holding the staff who hold the parents in the NICU. *Psychoanalytic Dialogues* 16(1): 149–164.

Kraemer, S., & Steinberg, Z. (2006) It's rarely cold in the NICU: The permeability of psychic space. *Psychoanalytic Dialogues* 16(1): 165–180.

Krystal, H. (1988) *Integration and Self Healing: Affect, Trauma, Alexithymia.* Hillsdale, NJ: The Analytic Press.

Kumar, M. (2012) The poverty in psychoanalysis: "Poverty" of psychoanalysis? *Psychology and Developing Societies* 24(1): 1–34.

Kupers, T. (1990) Public therapy in the nineties: Too tough cases, too few resources, too little time. *New Directions for Mental Health Services* 46(Summer): 101–111.

Kupers, T. (1999) *Prison Madness: The Mental Health Crisis Behind Bars and What We Must Do About It.* San Francisco: Jossey-Bass.

Kurin, R. (1984) Morality, personhood, and the exemplary life: Popular conceptions of Muslims in Paradise. In: B. D. Metcalf (Ed.), *Moral Conduct and Authority: The Place of Adab in South Asian Islam* (pp. 196–220). Berkeley: University of California Press.

Kusche, C. A. (2002) Psychoanalysis as prevention: Using PATHS to enhance ego development, object relationships, and cortical integration in children. *Journal of Applied Psychoanalytic Studies* 4(3): 283–302.

Lacan, J. (1972) *Ecrits.* A. Sheridan (Trans.). New York: Norton.

Laskey, A. L., Stump, T. E., Perkins, S. M., Zimet, G. D., Sherman, S. J., & Downs, S. M. (2012) Influence of race and socioeconomic status on the diagnosis of child abuse: A randomized study. *Journal of Pediatrics* 160(6): 1003–1008.

Layton, L. (2006) Racial identities, racial enactments, and normative unconscious processes. *The Psychoanalytic Quarterly* 75(1): 237–269.

Leblanc, A. N. (2003) *Random Family: Love, Drugs, Trouble, and Coming of Age.* New York: Scribner.

Levack, B. (2006) *The Witch-Hunt in Early Modern Europe.* London: Longman.

Linden, M. (2010) Budget cuts set funding path to historic lows. Retrieved from the Center for American Progress: http://americanprogress.org/wp-content/uploads/2013/01/LindenNonDefenseDiscretionarySpending.pdf

Loewald, H. (1979) The waning of the Oedipus complex. *Journal of the American Psychoanalytic Association* 27: 751–775.

Mahbubani, K. (2013) The closing of the Indian mind. In: C. Chandler & A. Zainulbhai (Eds.), *Reimagining India* (pp. 352–356). New York: Simon and Schuster.

Mahler, M. S., Pine, F., & Bergman, A. (1975) *The Psychological Birth of the Human Infant.* New York: Basic Books.

Maiello, S. (1999) Encounter with an African healer. *Journal of Child Psychotherapy* 25(2): 217–238.

Main, M., & Hesse, E. (1990) Parents unresolved traumatic experiences are related to infant disorganized attachment status: Is frightened and/or frightening parental behavior the linking mechanism? In: M. Greenberg, D. Ciccheti, & E. M. Cummings (Eds.), *Attachment in the Preschool Years: Theory, Research, and Intervention* (pp. 161–184). Chicago: University of Chicago Press.

Makari, G. (2008) *Revolution in Mind.* New York: Harper-Collins.

Malberg, N. (2008) Refusing to be excluded: Finding ways of integrating psychotherapeutic modalities to the emerging needs of a Pupil Referral Unit. *Journal of Child Psychotherapy* 34(1): 101–110.

Malik, J. (1998) The literary critique of Islamic popular religion in the guise of traditional mysticism, or the abused woman. In: P. Werbner & H. Basu (Eds.), *Embodying Charisma: Modernity, Locality, and the Performance of Emotion in Sufi Cults* (pp. 187–208). London and New York: Routledge.

Maltby, J. (2008) Consultation in schools: Helping staff and pupils with unresolved loss and mourning. *Journal of Child Psychotherapy* 34(1): 83–100.

Marans, S. (2004) Psychoanalytic responses to violent trauma: The child development-community policing partnership. In: B. Sklarew, W. Twemlow, & S. Wilkinson (Eds.), *Analysts in the Trenches: Streets, Schools, and War Zones* (pp. 211–236). Hillsdale, NJ: The Analytic Press.

Mazumdar-Shaw, K. (2013) Betting big on bio. In: C. Chandler & A. Zainulbhai (Eds.), *Reimagining India* (pp. 166–169). New York: Simon and Schuster.

McHugo, G. J., Drake, R. E., Teague, G. B., & Xie, H. (1999) Fidelity to assertive community treatment and client outcomes in the New Hampshire dual disorders study. *Psychiatric Services* 50(6): 818–824.

McNichol, E. (2012) Out of balance: Cuts in services have been states' primary response to budget gaps, harming the nation's economy. Retrieved from Center on Budget and Policy Priorities: http://www.cbpp.org/files/4–18–12sfp.pdf

McWilliams, N. (2011) *Psychoanalytic Diagnosis: Understanding Personality Structure in the Clinical Process.* Second Edition. New York: Guilford.

Menzies-Lyth, I.E.P. (1975) A case study in the functioning of social systems as a defense against anxiety. In: A. D. Colman & W. H. Bexton (Eds.), *Group Relations Reader I* (pp. 281–312). Jupiter, FL: A.K. Rice Institute.

Menzies-Lyth, I. (1985) Development of the self in children in institutions. In: I. Menzies-Lyth (Ed.), *Containing Anxieties in Institutions: Selected Essays* (pp. 236–258). London. Free Association Books.

Mesmer, F. A. (1814) Mesmerismus oder System der Wechsel-beziehungen. Theorie und Andwendungen des tierischen Magnetismus ("Mesmerism or the system of inter-relations. Theory and applications of animal magnetism" / original language: German). Berlin.

Mishel, L., Bivens, J., Gould, E., & Shierholz, H. (2012) *Economic Policy Institute's The State of Working America.* Twelfth Edition. Ithaca, NY: Cornell University Press.

Mitchell, S. A. (1988) *Relational Concepts in Psychoanalysis: An Integration.* New York: Basic Books.

Mitchell, S. A. (1993) *Hope and Dread in Psychoanalysis.* New York: Basic Books.

Mitchell, S. A. (1997) *Influence and Autonomy in Psychoanalysis.* Hillsdale, NJ: The Analytic Press.

Moi, T. (1995) Representations of patriarchy: sexuality and epistemology in Freud's Dora. In: C. Berheimer & C. Kahane (Eds.), *In Dora's Case: Freud-Hysteria-Feminism* (pp. 181–199). New York: Columbia University Press.

Morita, S. (1998) *Morita Therapy and the True Nature of Anxiety-Based Disorders (Shinkeishitsu).* Albany, NY: State University of New York Press.

Music, G., & Hall, B. (2008) From scapegoating to thinking and finding a home: Delivering therapeutic work in schools. *Journal of Child Psychotherapy* 34(1): 43–61.

Nelson, A. (2005) *The Combination.* New Orleans, LA: Red Rattle Books/Soft Skull Press.

Obeyesekere, G. (1978) Illness, culture, and meaning: Some comments on the nature of traditional medicine. In: A. Kleinman, P. Kunstadter, E. R. Alexander, & J. L. Gayle (Eds.), *Culture and Healing in Asian Societies* (pp. 253–263). Cambridge, MA: Schenkman.

Obholzer, A., & Roberts, E. Z., Eds. (1994) *The Unconscious at Work.* London: Routledge.

Osofsky, H. J., & Osofsky, J. D. (2004) Children's exposure to community violence: Psychoanalytic perspectives on evaluation and treatment. In: B. Sklarew, S. Twemlow, & S. Wilkinson (Eds.), *Analysts in the Trenches: Streets, Schools, War Zones* (pp. 237–256). Hillsdale, NJ: The Analytic Press.

Patel, V. (2002) *Where There is No Psychiatrist.* London: Gaskill.

Pfleiderer, B. (2006) *The Red Thread: Healing Possession at a Muslim Shrine in North India.* Delhi: Aakar Books.

Piketty, T., & Saez, E. (2003) Income inequality in the United States 1913–1998. *Quarterly Journal of Economics* 118(1): 1–39. Updated to 2011.

Piff, P. K. (2013) Wealth and the inflated self: Class, entitlement, and narcissism. *Personality and Social Psychology Bulletin* 40(1): 34–43.

Piff, P. K., Stancato, D. M., Martinez, A. G., Kraus, M. W., & Keltner, D. (2012) Class, chaos, and the construction of community. *Journal of Personality and Social Psychology* 103(6): 949–962.

Platts, J. T. (1983) *A Dictionary of Urdu, Classical Hindi, and English.* New Delhi: Munshiram Manoharlal Publishers.

Rank, O. (1936) Will Therapy and Truth and Reality. New York: Knopf.

Reeves, C. (1979) Transference in the residential treatment of children. *Journal of Child Psychotherapy* 5(1): 25–37.

Ringstrom, P. (2007) Scenes that write themselves: Improvisational moments in Relational Psychoanalysis. *Psychoanalytic Dialogues: The International Journal of Relational Perspectives* 17(1): 69–99.

Roland, A. (1988) *In Search of Self in India and Japan: Toward a Cross Cultural Psychology.* Princeton, NJ: Princeton University Press.

Roth, M. (2001) Falling into history: Freud's case of Emmy no N. In: M. Dimen & A. Harris (Eds.), *Storms in Her Head: Freud and the Construction of Hysteria* (pp. 167–184). New York: Other Press.

Sacramone, A. M. (2012) Free Association in the Width of the Square; Building a Community Model for Developmental Change from Recognition and Responsivity. Presented at the International Association for Psychoanalytic Self Psychology conference, Washington, D.C. October 18, 2012.

Safran, J., Ed. (2003) *Psychoanalysis and Buddhism: An Unfolding Dialogue.* Boston: Wisdom Publications.

Saheb, S.A.A. (1998) A 'festival of flags:' Hindu-Muslim devotion and the sacralizing of localism at the Nagore-e-Sharif in Tamil Nadu. In: P. Werbner & H. Basu (Eds.), *Embodying Charisma: Modernity, Locality, and the Performance of Emotion in Sufi Cults* (pp. 55–76). London and New York: Routledge.

Salovey, P., Rothman, A. J., Detweiler, J. B., & Steward, W. T. (2000) Emotional states and physical health. *American Psychologist* 55(1): 110–121.

Sarason, S. B., Levine, M., Goldenberg, I. I., Cherlin, D. L., & Bennett, E. M. (1966) *Psychology in Community Settings.* New York: Wiley.

Searles, H. (1965) *Collected Papers on Schizophrenia and Related Subjects.* New York: International Universities Press.

Sennett, R., & Cobb, J. (1972) *The Hidden Injuries of Class.* New York: Vintage Books.

Shepard, M. J. (2002) Consultant or comrade: Comments on analysts' working relationships in schools. *Journal of Applied Psychoanalytic Studies* 4(3): 331–338.

Sheppard, D. (2001) Clinical social work (1880–1940) and relational psychoanalysis: An historical interpretive analysis of relational concepts and practice. Unpublished doctoral dissertation, New York University.

Sigerist, H. E. (1948) The story of tarantism. In: D. Schullian & M. Schoen (Eds.), *Music and Medicine* (pp. 96–117). New York: Henry Schuman.

Silverman, M. (2002) Discussion: Application of psychoanalytic developmental understanding to three early intervention programs. *Journal of Applied Psychoanalytic Studies* 4(3): 339–346.

Sklarew, B., Handel, S., and Ley, S. (2012) The analyst at the Morgue: Helping families deal with traumatic bereavement. *Psychoanalytic Inquiry* 32(2): 147–157.

Sklarew, B., Krupnick, J., Ward-Wimmer, D., & Napoli, C. (2002) The school-based mourning project: A preventive intervention in the cycle of inner-city violence. *Journal of Applied Psychoanalytic Studies* 4(3): 317–330.

Skultans, V. (1987) The management of mental illness among Maharashtrian families: A case study of a Mahanubhav healing temple. *Man* 22(4): 661–679.

Smaller, M. (2012) Psychoanalysis and the forward edge hit the streets: The analytic services to adolescents program. *Psychoanalytic Inquiry* 32(2): 132–146.

Smith, L., & Thelen, E., Eds. (1993) *A dynamic Systems Approach to Development: Applications.* Cambridge, MA: MIT Press.

Spiro, M. E. (1978) Supernaturally caused illness in traditional Burmese medicine. In: A. Kleinman, P. Kunstadter, E. R. Alexander, & J. L. Gayle (Eds.), *Culture and Healing in Asian Societies* (pp. 219–234). Cambridge, MA: Schenkman.

Spitz, R. A. (1965) *The First Year of Life: A Psychoanalytic Study of Normal and Deviant Development of Object Relations.* New York: International Universities Press.

Sprince, J. (2000) Towards an integrated network. *Journal of Child Psychotherapy* 26(3): 413–431.

Sprince, J. (2002) Developing containment: Psychoanalytic consultancy to a therapeutic community for traumatized children. *Journal of Child Psychotherapy* 28(2): 147–161.

Stanton, A. M., & Schwartz, M. (1954) *The Mental Hospital.* New York: Basic Books.

Stein, L. I., & Santos, A. B. (1998) *Assertive Community Treatment of Persons with Severe Mental Illness.* New York and London: W.W. Norton.

Steinberg, Z. (2006) Pandora meets the NICU parent, or whither hope? *Psychoanalytic Dialogues* 16(1): 131–148.

Steptoe, A., & Molloy, G. J. (2007) Personality and heart disease. *Heart* 93(7): 783–784.

Stern, D. B. (2002) Language and the non-verbal as a unity: Discussion of "Where is the action in the talking cure." *Contemporary Psychoanalysis* 38(3): 515–525.

Stern, D. N. (1985) *The Interpersonal World of the Infant: A View from Psychoanalysis and Developmental Psychology.* New York: Basic Books.

Stiglitz, J. E. (2003) *Globalization and Its Discontents.* New York and London: W.W. Norton.

Substance Abuse and Mental Health Services Administration. (2008) *Assertive Community Treatment: Getting Started with EBPs.* DHHS Pub. No. SMA-08–4344, Rockville, MD: Center for Mental Health Services, Substance Abuse and Mental Health Services Administration, U.S. Department of Health and Human Services Administration, U.S. Department of Health and Human Services.

Sullivan, H. S. (1953) *The Interpersonal Theory of Psychiatry.* NY: Norton.

Sutton, A. (2002) Psychoanalytic psychotherapy in pediatric liaison: A diagnostic and therapeutic tool. *Journal of Child Psychotherapy* 28(2): 181–200.

Trungpa, C. (1973) *Cutting Through Spiritual Materialism.* Boston: Shambhala Publications.

Tseng, W. S. (1978) Traditional and modern psychiatric care in Taiwan. In: A. Kleinman, P. Kunstadter, E. R. Alexander, & J. L. Gate (Eds.), *Culture and Healing in Asian Societies: Anthropological, Psychiatric, and Public Health Studies* (pp. 311–328). Cambridge: Schenkman Publishing Company.

Twemlow, S., & Wilkinson, S. M. (2004) Topeka's Healthy Community Initiative. In: B. Sklarew, S. W. Twemlow, & S. M. Wilkinson (Eds.), *Analysts in the Trenches* (pp. 103–136). Hillsdale, NJ: The Analytic Press.

Twemlow, S. (2013) Broadening the vision; a community-based psychoanalysis in the context of usual practice. *Journal of the American Psychoanalytic Association* 61(4): 662–690.

Wachtel, P. L. (1989) *The Poverty of Affluence.* Philadelphia, PA and Santa Cruz, CA: New Society Publishers.

Weisbrod, B. A., Test, M. A., & Stein, L. I. (1980) Alternative to mental hospital treatment II: Economic benefit-cost analysis. *Archives of General Psychiatry* 37: 400–405.

Werbner, P. (1998) LANGAR: Pilgrimage, sacred exchange and perpetual sacrifice in a Sufi saint's lodge. In: P. Werbner & H. Basu (Eds.), *Embodying Charisma: Modernity, Locality, and the Performance of Emotion in Sufi Cults* (pp. 95–116). London and New York: Routledge.

Winnicott, D. W. (1956) Primary maternal preoccupation. In: *Through Pediatrics to Psychoanalysis* (pp. 300–305). New York: Basic Books. Republished in 1975.

Winnicott, D. W. (1969) The use of an object and relating through identifications. In: *Playing and Reality* (pp. 86–94). London: Tavistock. Republished in 1971.

Winnicott, D. W. (1971) *The Maturational Processes and the Facilitating Environment.* New York: International Universities Press.

Winnicott, D. W. (1986) *Holding and Interpretation: Fragment of an Analysis.* London: Karnac.

# Index

Made in the USA
San Bernardino, CA
09 July 2018